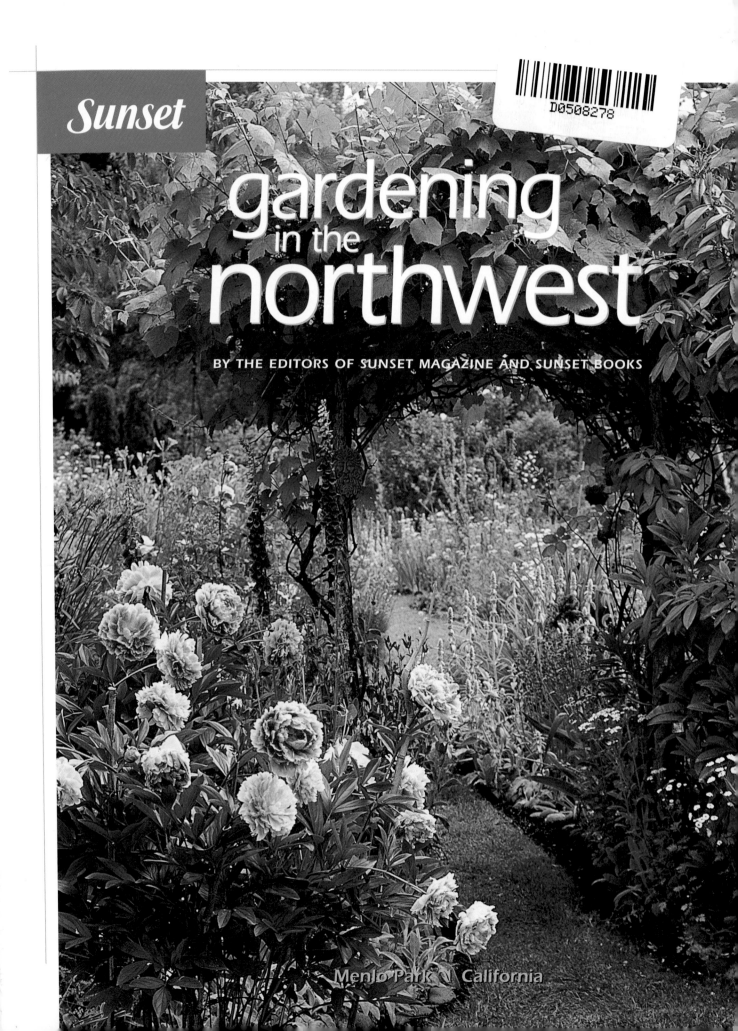

Sunset

gardening
in the
northwest

BY THE EDITORS OF SUNSET MAGAZINE AND SUNSET BOOKS

Menlo Park ✦ California

SUNSET BOOKS

Vice President, General Manager: Richard A. Smeby
Vice President, Editorial Director: Bob Doyle
Production Director: Lory Day
Director of Operations: Rosann Sutherland
Sales Development Director: Linda Barker
Art Director: Vasken Guiragossian

Staff for this book:
Editor: Kathleen Norris Brenzel
Managing Editor: Fiona Gilsenan
Art Director: Alice Rogers
Senior Editors: Steven R. Lorton, Jim McCausland
Assistant Editor: Susan M. Guthrie
Copy Editor: Elissa Rabellino
Senior Writers: Valerie Easton, Debra Prinzing
Contributing Writers: Barbara Ashmun, Carol Hall,
     Mary-Kate Mackay, Christina Pfeiffer

Proofreaders: Barbara J. Braasch, Christine Miklas
Indexer: Erin Hartshorn
Production Coordinator: Danielle Javier

Photo Editor: Cynthia del Fava
Page Production: Linda M. Bouchard
Map Illustration: Jane Shasky
Illustration: Connie McLennan

Cover: Photography by Paddy Wales.
Garden design by Brian Clarke.

10 9 8 7 6 5 4 3 2 1
First printing January 2003
Copyright © 2003 Sunset Publishing Corporation, Menlo Park, CA 94025.
First edition. All rights reserved, including the right of reproduction
in whole or in part in any form.
Library of Congress Control Number: 2002113832. ISBN 0-376-03528-5.

Printed in the United States.

For additional copies of *Gardening in the Northwest*
or any other Sunset book, call 1-800-526-5111 or visit us at
www.sunsetbooks.com

contents

dedication

LOCALS SOMETIMES REFER TO WESTERN OREGON, WASHINGTON, AND LOWER BRITISH COLUMBIA AS CASCADIA, SUGGESTING A LAND APART.

In many ways, this beautiful region, bordered on the west by the Pacific Ocean and on the east by the Cascade range, is just that. It's lush, lovely, and—where lakes, rivers, or Puget Sound moderate the climate—one of the best places on earth to tend a garden.

But Cascadia is just one part of the Northwest. Here, as east of the Cascades and in Alaska, gardeners find inspiration in the majestic natural landscape, using snow-capped mountains, pastoral valleys, moss-draped forests, or scenic waterways as backdrops. They draw design ideas from native peoples, and those who came from afar. At the same time, Northwesterners approach gardening with rugged individualism, turning house-boats, roof decks, and sandy beaches into magical spaces.

Something else draws together these places: a collective con-science that urges care for the land. To conserve water during dry summers, many residents willingly let their lawns go brown. To keep waterways safe for migrating salmon, thoughtful gardeners curb runoff of water and chemicals by using porous paving, which allows water to percolate though it, and by improving the soil with compost to filter out pollutants.

The Master Gardener Program got its start in Washington's King and Pierce counties, becoming an international force for good gardening. Seattle Tilth, a nonprofit organic gardening group, introduced the first citywide composting program. And Northwest designers constantly invent fresh ways to recycle materials like wood, glass, and plastic.

We dedicate this book to all gardeners who work to make a slice of Northwest soil the best it can be. It's our hope that the ideas in these pages from fellow Northwesterners will enrich your gardening experience.

—KATHLEEN N. BRENZEL
Senior Garden Editor

STEVEN R. LORTON, Seattle JIM McCAUSLAND, Port Orchard, WA
FIONA GILSENAN, Victoria, B.C.

n

orthwest

introduction

THIS IS A REMARKABLE REGION. *Canadians call it the Southwest; Americans call it the Northwest. But on both sides of the border the rainy parts are known as Cascadia, and the rest just "the dry side of the mountains." Your garden may be cold enough to grow apples, peaches, and cherries, or warm enough to ripen impossibly sweet melons and corn. It may be lashed by Pacific storms, or soaked with so much sun that grapes burst with flavor, and roses bloom over and over. You may garden nearly year-round, or for just a few short but glorious months.* ❧ *Early seafaring visitors were appalled at the wind and rain. Spanish settlers struggled with it during their 5-month stay on the Olympic Peninsula. Writing from makeshift Fort Clatsop in Astoria, Meriwether Lewis recorded only 12 rainless days from November 5, 1804, through March 25, 1805. Seattle's first settlers left Alki Point for the shelter of big trees (and a deep harbor) east of Elliott Bay, where the city now stands.* ❧ *But for modern gardeners, even the inclement weather has its magic. Breezes animate everything from aspens to ornamental grasses, raindrops turn winter moss iridescent, and rhododendrons and ferns grow better in our moist woodland shade than almost anywhere else.*

northwest climate zones

| 1A |
| 2A |
| 2B |
| 3A |
| 3B |
| 4 |
| 5 |
| 6 |
| 7 |
| 17 |

For Alaskan zones, please see page 16

Campbell River

Kelowna

2A

Vancouver · Hope

1A

4 · Fraser River

Nanaimo

4

1A · Bellingham

5

Victoria

5

Forks · Port Angeles

Okanagan River

Creston

2B

Sandpoint

Omak

1A

2A

Coeur d'Alene

3B

Everett

4

Seattle

Spokane

2B

2A

Hoquiam · Tacoma

Wenatchee

Olympia · Ellensburg

Moses Lake

Long Beach

5 · 4

2B

Yakima

3B

3A

Longview

2B

3B

Astoria

Walla Walla

Lewiston

3A

4

2A

2B

Columbia River

Tri-Cities

Portland

3A · The Dalles

Hood River

3B

3A · Pendleton

2A

2B · La Grande

Willamette River

Lincoln City

Salem

5 · 6

2A

Baker

Snake River

4

Eugene

Bend

2B

Reedsport

Boise

Coos Bay

3A

4 · Roseburg

1A · Burns

Rogue River

Gold Beach

1A · 7 · Medford

Grants Pass

2A

Klamath Falls

17

The Sunset Western Garden Book assigns climate zones to every listed plant. We divide the Northwest into 10 broad climate zones (and a further three in Alaska), but the story doesn't stop there. For more detailed information on climate influences in your area, turn to the maps on the following pages.

The Coast Range, which runs from the Siskiyous to the Olympics, faces the great, mild ocean during summer and bears the brunt of its ferocious storms during winter. Cool summers make it a challenge to ripen

coastal strip

tomatoes and corn but also stretch out the bloom season for all kinds of perennials. Abundant rain nurtures rhododendrons and hardy fuchsias along the edges of the vast rain forest. Properties blessed with streams, springs, or bogs can produce world-class candelabra primroses, and even muck-loving but pristine yellow skunk cabbages and carnivorous *Darlingtonia californica*.

Gardeners soon discover why there are so many kite shops on the coast: The wind is constant. The closer you live to the ocean, the more the wind-blown sea salt burns your plants. Protect them by installing windbreaks, or build a gravel path and sow some low-growing annuals, like wonderful Popsicle-colored Livingstone daisies.

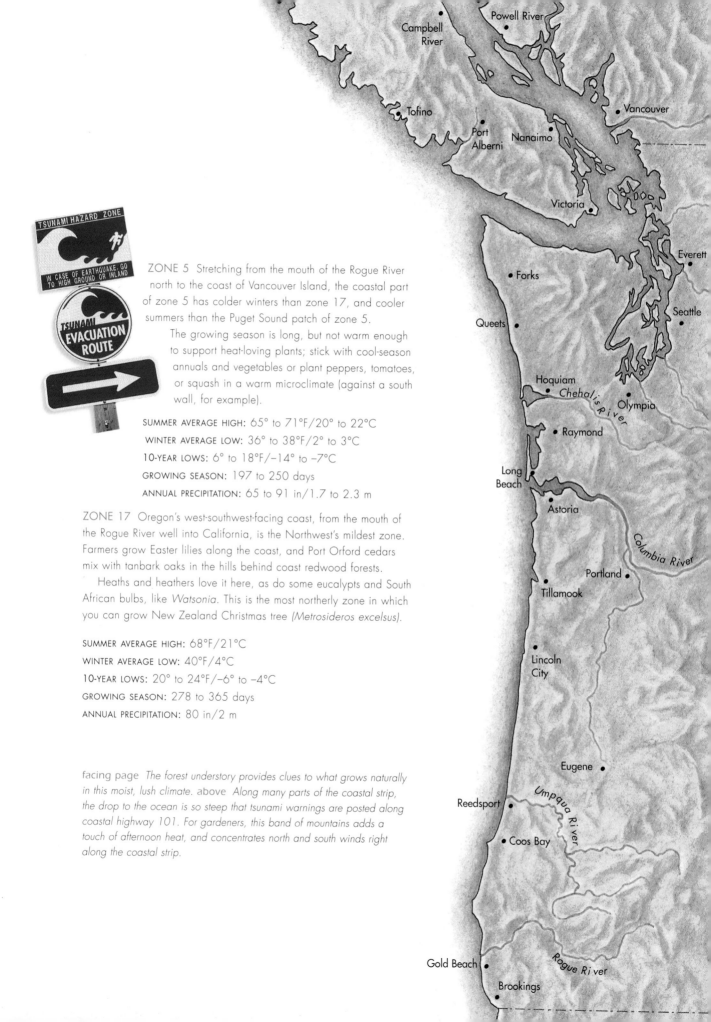

ZONE 5 Stretching from the mouth of the Rogue River north to the coast of Vancouver Island, the coastal part of zone 5 has colder winters than zone 17, and cooler summers than the Puget Sound patch of zone 5.

The growing season is long, but not warm enough to support heat-loving plants; stick with cool-season annuals and vegetables or plant peppers, tomatoes, or squash in a warm microclimate (against a south wall, for example).

SUMMER AVERAGE HIGH: 65° to 71°F/20° to 22°C
WINTER AVERAGE LOW: 36° to 38°F/2° to 3°C
10-YEAR LOWS: 6° to 18°F/−14° to −7°C
GROWING SEASON: 197 to 250 days
ANNUAL PRECIPITATION: 65 to 91 in/1.7 to 2.3 m

ZONE 17 Oregon's west-southwest-facing coast, from the mouth of the Rogue River well into California, is the Northwest's mildest zone. Farmers grow Easter lilies along the coast, and Port Orford cedars mix with tanbark oaks in the hills behind coast redwood forests.

Heaths and heathers love it here, as do some eucalypts and South African bulbs, like *Watsonia*. This is the most northerly zone in which you can grow New Zealand Christmas tree (*Metrosideros excelsus*).

SUMMER AVERAGE HIGH: 68°F/21°C
WINTER AVERAGE LOW: 40°F/4°C
10-YEAR LOWS: 20° to 24°F/−6° to −4°C
GROWING SEASON: 278 to 365 days
ANNUAL PRECIPITATION: 80 in/2 m

facing page *The forest understory provides clues to what grows naturally in this moist, lush climate.* above *Along many parts of the coastal strip, the drop to the ocean is so steep that tsunami warnings are posted along coastal highway 101. For gardeners, this band of mountains adds a touch of afternoon heat, and concentrates north and south winds right along the coastal strip.*

In spring of 1792, Captain George Vancouver sailed down the Strait of
Juan de Fuca and into a remarkable inland sea. White-flowered dogwoods
and pink rhododendrons lined the shores, and the waters
were dotted with the fabulous archipelago of the San Juan
and Gulf Islands.

inland
sea

Clearly smitten with the beauty of the place, Vancouver
wrote in his journal on May 19, 1792, "To describe this
region, will, on some future occasion, be a very grateful task. The serenity
of the climate, the innumerable pleasing landscapes, and the abundant fertility, require only to be enriched by the industry of man." This may seem a
touch optimistic, but, in fact, he accurately predicted the range of horticultural possibilities. Now, cottage and Japanese gardens abound, as do some
of the world's finest public gardens and parks. Much of this wealth lies on
the Canadian side of the border, in such places as The Butchart Gardens,
the Horticulture Centre
of the Pacific, the VanDusen
Botanical Garden, Minter
Gardens, and the University
of British Columbia Botanical
Garden.

Around Puget Sound to
the south, the climate warms
and gardens crowd the shore.
Underlying glacial till is a
problem that gardeners over-
come with persistent rock-
picking and soil amendment.

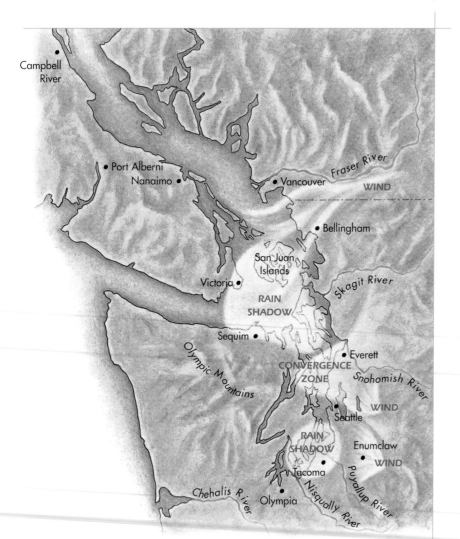

*On cold winter days, freezing air
flows down the Fraser River Valley
and over Cascade passes, creating
ice storms and cold winds in Cascadia.
A relatively arid rain shadow lies
between the Olympic Mountains and
the San Juan Islands; in summer, it shifts
down over Puget Sound. In spring,
Pacific storms divide around the
Olympics, then converge near Seattle,
dousing the region with rain.*

ZONE 4. With the exception of milder patches of zone 5 in the Victoria area, on Whidbey and Fidalgo islands, and the border of most of Puget Sound, most of the gardens here are in zone 4.

If you garden from Everett north, or more than a few miles from Puget Sound, Lake Washington, or Lake Sammamish, you're probably thankful to be in this zone. It's the most dependable northwestern Washington climate for ripening corn. Northern highbush blueberries are sensational here, as are spring-blooming bulbs and flowering trees. But the Cascades foothills occasionally experience intense local winter winds; you can help evergreens by windowing them to let winds blow through.

SUMMER AVERAGE HIGH: 71° to 79°F/21° to 26°C
WINTER AVERAGE LOW: 30° to 33°F/−1° to 1°C
10-YEAR LOWS: 0° to 5° F/−17° to −15°C
GROWING SEASON: 165 to 200 days
ANNUAL PRECIPITATION: 32 to 69 in/81 cm to 1.7 m

ZONE 5 is more favorable for gardening around Puget Sound than it is along the coastal strip (see page 9). Summer temperatures are higher in Seattle than in Hoquaim, for example, and winter lows are colder. There's also far less wind around the Sound. Surprisingly, Chinese windmill palms grow better here than they do in Southern California, and Korean dogwoods thrive.

That locally famous convergence zone, which centers on the King/Snohomish county line and extends east to the Cascades, supplies an extra inch of rain per month in April and May.

SUMMER AVERAGE HIGH: 72° to 77°F/22° to 25°C
ANNUAL PRECIPITATION: 17 to 51 in/43 cm to 1.3 m

above Alpine parks explode with color in summer. Here, on Hurricane Ridge, Indian paintbrush and lupines cloak a slope. The snowy peaks of the Olympic Mountains block much of the Pacific rainfall from reaching Puget Sound. On the south and west sides of the mountains, up to 150 in/3.8 m of rain can fall; in the rain shadow at Sequim, the average is 18 in/45 cm.

columbia river basin

The earliest settlers knew it well: With abundant heat and sunshine, all the low-elevation Columbia River Basin needed was water to grow nearly anything. But the annual rainfall was only 7 to 19 inches/18 to 48 centimeters. Today "anything" grows: melons, apples, peppers, trumpet vines, and lilacs, for starters.

Water did it. In the late 1830s, settlers started irrigating land around Walla Walla, which had the longest growing season (over 200 days) in the Northwestern interior. By the early 1950s, President Roosevelt's Columbia Basin Irrigation Project was bringing water to thousands of square miles that today sustain most of Washington's orchards, farms, and vineyards.

ZONE 2b. An area with well-defined seasons and much wind. In many gardens, windbreaks are vital.

SUMMER AVERAGE HIGH:
84° to 89°F/29° to 32°C
WINTER AVERAGE LOW:
18° to 24°F/−8° to −4°C
10-YEAR LOWS:
−15° to −21°F/−26° to −29°C
GROWING SEASON: 135 to 180 days
ANNUAL PRECIPITATION: 9 to 19 in/
23 to 48 cm

ZONE 3b. The mildest interior climate is perfect for melons, corn, peppers, tomatoes, and fruits (like apples, cherries, peaches, pears, and even American persimmons).

SUMMER AVERAGE HIGH:
85° to 91°F/29° to 32°C
WINTER AVERAGE LOW:
22° to 28°F/−5° to −2°C
10-YEAR LOWS:
−5° to −15°F/−20° to −26°C
GROWING SEASON: 180 to 210 days
ANNUAL PRECIPITATION: 8 to 19 in/
20 to 48 cm

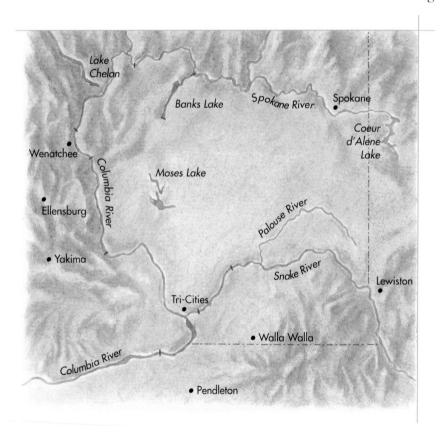

columbia river basin map *Roughly ringed by the Columbia and Snake Rivers, the low-elevation Columbia River Basin is surrounded on all sides by mountains. It is naturally dry and hot in summer, and for the most part the land is treeless and subject to steady winds that stunt plants unless they are protected. Eleven hydroelectric dams supply the region with power, and several feed into an extensive irrigation system that makes the land productive.*

rogue river valley map *Easily among the hottest summer regions in the state, the interior of this valley is at a fairly low elevation (1,000 to 1,750 ft/305 to 533 m above sea level) and is not subject to the ocean's moderating influence due to the mountains to the west. Winters are cold, but rarely does the ground freeze—exactly how many fruits and deciduous ornamentals like it.*

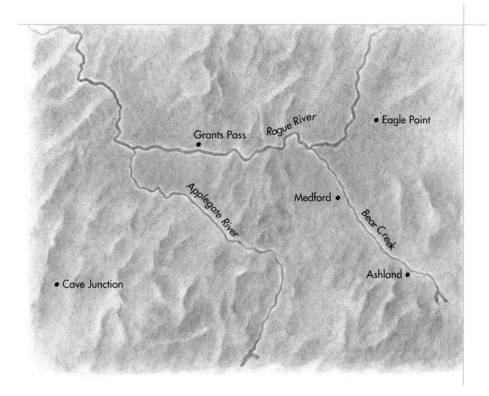

Dotted with buttes and surrounded by corrugated mountains and extinct volcanoes, Southern Oregon's Rogue River Valley is home to legions of gardeners. Vernal pools abound (see good ones in spring atop Black Butte), and nearby mountains are home to rare native plants like Brewer's weeping spruce. Commercial rose growers have bases here, as do singular specialty nurseries such as Forestfarm and Siskiyou Rare Plant Nursery.

rogue river valley

The land tends to be dry; its native trees are mostly Oregon white oaks, ponderosa pines, and incense cedars, often with poison oak growing beneath. But remarkable gardens grow wherever people till the soil; if you have water to spare, you can fill the garden with roses, clematis, and cottage-garden flowers. The Rogue River is also home to some of the West's finest rock gardens, orchards, and vineyards.

ZONE 7. Centered on the Rogue River Valley from Medford to Grant's Pass, this zone also takes in tributary valleys from all directions. Plant deciduous shade trees to moderate the hot summer sun around the garden; although the growing season is not long, nearly any warm-season crop will mature.

SUMMER AVERAGE HIGH: 86° to 90°F/30° to 32°C
WINTER AVERAGE LOW: 21° to 32°F/−6° to 0°C
10-YEAR LOWS: 0° to 10°F/−18° to −12°C
GROWING SEASON: 150 to 175 days
ANNUAL PRECIPITATION: 19 to 61 in/48 to 155 cm

western oregon

With their rich soil, chilly winters, and warm summers, western Oregon's well-watered river valleys can grow a phenomenal range of plants, from hazelnuts and berries to tree fruits, grapes, rhododendrons, and the Umpqua River Valley's legendary melons. The Willamette Valley's world-class nursery and greenhouse industry ranks first in Oregon's agriculture.

Most of this region is tucked between the Coast Range and the Cascades, from the Umpqua River Valley north through the fertile Willamette to the Cowlitz River Valley in southwest Washington. The mountain ranges moderate Pacific storms for the valleys that lie to the east, but blasts of winter cold rush west to Portland through the Columbia River Gorge, freezing tender plants. Visit the Oregon Garden in Silverton to see firsthand how things grow here.

ZONE 6
SUMMER AVERAGE HIGH: 79° to 83°F/26° to 28°C
WINTER AVERAGE LOW: 30° to 36°F/−1° to 2°C
10-YEAR LOWS: 0° to 12°F/−18 to −11°C
GROWING SEASON: 150 to 225 days
ANNUAL PRECIPITATION: 34 to 54 in/85 to 162 cm

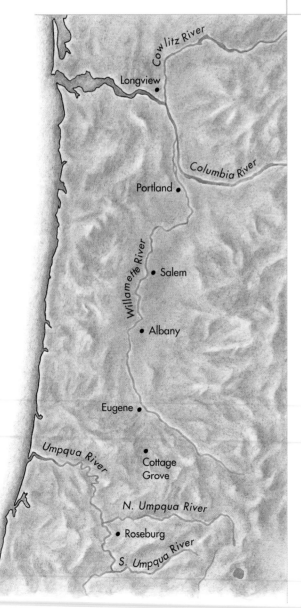

western oregon map Hills and small mountain ranges modify the climate in much of the Willamette Valley. On their southern and western slopes are planted some of the world's finest 'Pinot Noir' vineyards, while the cooler, often-forested north slopes are better for woodland gardens. Valley bottoms that once grew vast fields of native camass are now home to irises, grasses, and tulips destined to be shipped to gardens all over the country.

mountains and plains map Geographically, mountains separate the West from most of the continent. Mountain gardeners enjoy sharply divided seasons, often spectacular views, and the right habitat for growing a relatively wide range of alpine plants. The mountain climate zone is the largest in the Northwest.

In the Northwest mountains, north and east exposures stay cooler and hold snow longer; sunny south and west hillsides get hot on summer afternoons.

mountains and plains

Open ridges are colder in winter and windier all the time than the slopes below. Rocky mineral soil, dry air, and temperature drops of 30° to 40°F/17° to 22°C at night are common to most of these mountains, but precipitation varies.

Most Northwest storms start over the Pacific Ocean and blow east, over the Coast Range and Olympic Mountains, the Cascades, and finally the Rockies. Mountains nearest the ocean get the most precipitation overall, the wettest snow, and the mildest winter temperatures. East of the Cascades crest, there's so little moisture that even the snow usually falls as dry powder.

In all mountain ranges, rain and snow increase the higher up you are. The snow makes a great insulator and can keep many plants alive, as can a thick layer of pine needles or other organic mulch.

ZONE 1a

SUMMER AVERAGE HIGH: 80° to 87°F/26° to 30°C
WINTER AVERAGE LOW: 0° to 20°F/−18° to −7°C
10-YEAR LOWS: −20° to −35°F/−28° to −37°C
GROWING SEASON: 50 to 100 days
ANNUAL PRECIPITATION: 9 to 82 in/23 cm to 2 m

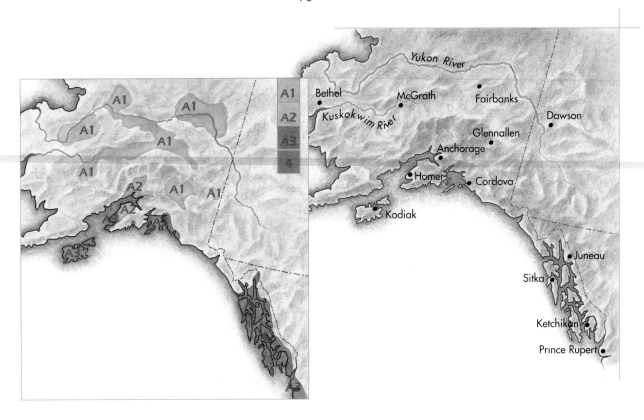

As any northerner can tell you, nothing dispels cabin fever better than gardening. Perhaps that's why Alaskans (and northern British Columbians) readily meet such challenges as 12 feet/3.6 meters of annual rainfall (in Ketchikan), 150°F/83°C summer-to-winter temperature swings (in Fairbanks), and ravenous moose (nearly everywhere). Alaska's corps of extension agents, and some excellent nurseries and botanical gardens, have significantly broadened the scope of what can be grown here, and helped make it one of the West's horticultural surprises.

alaska

ZONE A1. SUMMER AVERAGE HIGH: 68° to 73°F/20° to 23°C
WINTER AVERAGE LOW: −18° to −28°F/−28° to −33°C
10-YEAR LOWS: −60° to −68°F/−51° to −55°C
GROWING SEASON: 85 to 115 days
ANNUAL PRECIPITATION: 7 to 17 in/18 to 43 cm

ZONE A2. SUMMER AVERAGE HIGH: 62° to 65°F/17° to 18°C
WINTER AVERAGE LOW: 3° to 8°F/−16° to −13°C
10-YEAR LOWS: −30° to −45°F/−34° to −43°C
GROWING SEASON: 105 to 138 days
ANNUAL PRECIPITATION: 15 to 19 in/38 to 43 cm

ZONE A3. SUMMER AVERAGE HIGH: 61° to 68°F/16° to 19°C
WINTER AVERAGE LOW: 15° to 25°F/−9° to −4°C
10-YEAR LOWS: −2° to −22°F/−18° to −30°C
GROWING SEASON: 113 to 160 days
ANNUAL PRECIPITATION: 25 to 150 in/63 cm to 3.8 m

ZONE 4. SUMMER AVERAGE HIGH: 62° to 65°F/17° to 18°C
ANNUAL PRECIPITATION: 86 to 150 in/2.1 to 3.8 m

How can one gardener grow fragrant Mexican orange year after year, while a close neighbor invariably fails? Or why does one vegetable plot produce tomatoes until October, while another just down the street nearly always freezes two weeks earlier? The answers involve microclimates—small pockets on your property that are seasonally colder, warmer, or windier than the rest of the garden or neighborhood.

microclimates

❧ SLOPING GROUND allows cold air to drain downhill like water. This air stays a bit warmer than the still air on mountaintops above or valleys below. That's why sloping ground is favored for growing tender plants.

❧ COLD AIR POOLS in low spots. A solid hedge or fence can also dam up cold air. In the Northwest, this extra chill can freeze borderline-hardy plants but help high-chill plants.

❧ EXPOSURE TO WIND desiccates plants and stunts growth. A hedge or windbreak on the windward side can create a sheltered area extending 10 to 20 times its height.

❧ SOUTH AND WEST WALLS concentrate heat by reflecting sunlight. Masonry walls also soak up heat and radiate it back at night. In cool-summer areas, that heat can help ripen tomatoes. In hot-summer areas, you may want to shade or screen these walls.

❧ NORTH WALLS get little direct sun, so they are ideal for shade-loving plants like ferns.

❧ EAST WALLS bask in morning sun, but are sheltered from scorching afternoon sun—perfect for azaleas, fuchsias, and perennials that like plenty of light but not much heat.

❧ SHADE TREES and overhead structures cast filtered shade preferred by many plants. On frosty nights, the air beneath stays a few degrees warmer than open ground— a crucial difference for tender plants.

❧ OVERHANGING EAVES protect delicate flowers like camellias from rain and provide a few degrees of frost protection in winter.

prevailing wind

shade trees

N

sloping ground

cool-air pools

seasons

Seasons are not subtle in the Pacific Northwest. Winter is wet and chilly, with occasional snow, yet mild enough to allow broad-leafed evergreens to prosper. Over the mountains, winter is cold and often dry; so you must mulch to keep roots from heaving in frost.

Spring has mercurial weather and abundant blooms. Wind, sun, and drenching rain coax daffodils out of the ground on both sides of the mountains. By April Fool's Day, most deciduous trees are still bare. But by May Day, nearly everything has leafed out, and the growing season is under way. East of the Cascades, spring brings the best lilacs, celebrated in Spokane with a week-long festival in mid-May.

Summer is our dry season, as our brown lawns attest. But dry weather is a boon to tomato growers, and the long days and mild temperatures keep perennials and cool-season annuals flowering. On the east side, many places have enough heat to ripen watermelons and wine grapes.

Autumn nights become chilly in September, leaves start coloring up (but don't reach peak intensity until late October and early November on both sides of the mountains), and chrysanthemums, asters, and dahlias do for the flower border what pumpkins and corn do for the vegetable garden.

In Alaska, fall and winter come early, with birches turning golden as early as September. In Anchorage, the end of September brings 'termination dust'—the first snows, signalling to gardeners that it's time to hang up their tools for the winter.

top 10 challenges

Scott Conner knows a thing or two about gardening in the Northwest; he teaches horticulture, lectures widely, and hosts a weekend radio program "Gardening in the Northwest" (KOMO). We asked him which questions get lobbed his way most frequently. His answers:

❧ WHAT WORKS IN DRY SHADE? "See what's growing in the forest understory," advises Conner. "Salal, huckleberry, and vine maples are good choices. Or look at native perennials such as foamflowers and fringe flowers."

❧ HOW DO I KILL MOSS IN LAWNS? Too much shade (especially in winter), compacted, wet, or acid soil all encourage moss. Aerate and fertilize the lawn and check the soil pH; if it's too acid, mix in lime, rototill, and start over. "If all else fails, let the moss take over," advises Conner. "Let nature take its course. There's nothing wrong with a moss lawn."

❧ SHOULD I GROW MARGINALLY HARDY PLANTS? Temperatures that dip below 20°F/–6°C for a week or more are uncommon in milder areas. But some years, gardeners who grow marginally hardy plants flirt with disaster. Don't use such plants for hedges or other long-term plantings.

❧ WHAT'S THE BEST WAY TO CARE FOR BIG TREES? With safety in mind. Call in an arborist certified by the International Society of Arborists (ISA) to give you a

A moss lawn

"hazard appraisal" and to periodically thin and shape trees. Otherwise, check your trees regularly for dead branches, unusual foliage color, cavities or rotten wood, or cracks or splits where branches are attached. Pave beneath an established tree only with material that allows air and water to reach the tree roots.

❧ CAN I CURE TOMATO LATE BLIGHT? Prevention is the best cure. Late blight shows up around harvest time—"as soon as it rains," says Conner—causing spoiled leaves and rotted fruit. Avoid overhead watering; flood or drip-irrigate tomato plants; or cover rows with clear plastic. Choose early-ripening or resistant varieties. Provide good air circulation around plants, and clean up and destroy debris after harvest.

❧ WHAT'S THAT RED HAZE ON MY LAWN? It's red thread fungus (*Laetisaria fuciformis*), a disease common in wet climates. "I call it proof that aliens are here," says Conner. Red thread attacks stressed plants, particularly perennial ryegrass and some fescues. Control it with proper lawn care, and don't fertilize late in the season.

❧ YOU'RE KIDDING? DROUGHT IN THE NORTHWEST? "We know the big D is going to happen," says Conner, "we just don't know when. The Northwest has a finite supply of water, yet our population is growing." Conner's advice: Use drought-tolerant plants, install a drip irrigation system, and mulch to keep evaporation down.

❧ HELP! MY ENGLISH IVY'S RUNNING AMOK. Ivy can escape the backyard and run rampant; purple loosestrife (*Lythrum salicaria* and perhaps *L. virgatum*), have displaced native vegetation and choked wetlands. "Every year, hundreds of perennials and grasses come into the Northwest, and we don't always know at first how invasive they are," says Conner. Grow English ivy in a container on a patio or indoors. Planting *Lythrum* is unwise in moist areas.

❧ HOW DO I PRUNE MY HYDRANGEA? Prune a mophead after flowering (between November and February), making cuts back to wood that bloomed last year. To control the plant's size and shape, make cuts back to the strongest pair of new shoots, or to a pair of buds that will send out stems where you want new growth to be.

❧ AND A RHODIE? To encourage bushy growth, immediately after flowering pinch off faded trusses, but don't damage growth buds below the breaking point. To slightly reduce the plant's size, prune immediately after flowers fade. "I use the Italian method of pruning," says Conner. "Pinch out new growth, then cut errant branches. Works like a charm."

soils

Most of us think of soils as heavy (clay), medium-heavy (silt), or light (sand). Good loam is a blend of all three. It drains well, holds plenty of air, and has a pH in the 6 to 7 range.

Alas, such legendary loam is usually made, not found. Most gardens begin with native soil. Around Puget Sound, that may be glacial till (a mix of sand, rock, and clay); in broad, flat, river valleys, it is probably silt or clay; along much of the Oregon coast, it's often pure sand. To improve it, add a 3- to 4-inch/8- to 10-cm layer of organic matter. It helps light soil hold nutrients and water better, improves drainage and air-holding capacity of heavy soil, and increases beneficial biological activity in all soils. For other simple solutions, see facing page.

Such soil amendment makes sense in several situations. Do it annually in vegetable or high-performance flower gardens, where you're trying to grow plants for show or for production. Do it once when you're creating a first garden on extremely light or heavy soil, or on the subsoil left after a bulldozer has cleared and leveled the property for construction.

It doesn't make sense to do large-scale soil amendment in most other situations. Here's why.

Most unimproved garden soil can grow a wide range of permanent ornamental plants without amendment. Even difficult garden soils can support whole categories of plants. For example, you can grow *Gunnera,* Japanese iris, camass, and candelabra primrose in boggy ground; or many kinds of penstemon, agastache, sage, and pine in dry, poor soil. Coastal sand dunes support heaths, heathers, and some pines, while very acid soil is great for blueberries. Once you've considered the possibilities, you may not want to change your soil.

Where soil is impossibly rocky, hard, poorly drained, or chemically imbalanced, it can save grief in the long run to build raised beds, fill them with imported topsoil, and do most of your gardening there.

Boggy, acidic soils naturally support acid-lovers like lichen and cranberries.

designer dirt

So what do you do if your soil is poor? Nothing—if you carefully match your plants to your site. Or you could expand your gardening options by amending soil to adjust its pH, and adding organic matter to improve its fertility and texture. If your plants are still struggling, try one of these newer methods, devised to take soil improvement to a new level.

◥ SUPERSIZE YOUR COMPOST. It's well known that compost improves soil texture—improving drainage and helping plant roots breathe. But it also improves soil at a microscopic level that benefits plant growth. Surrounding plant roots is a complex web of bacteria, fungi, and other micro-organisms that help them absorb vital soil nutrients. Pesticides, fertilizers, and even tilling disrupt this fragile biological balance.

◥ CONCENTRATE THE BENEFITS OF COMPOST WITH A HOME COMPOST-TEA BREWER. These units combine compost (courtesy of a worm bin), water, and a nutrient solution, then aerate the mixture with a pump for 24 hours. With plenty of food and oxygen, the micro-organisms multiply to create a superrich compost "soup" that can be diluted and applied in and around plants to improve growth and disease-resistance. Research is under way to see whether these solutions may also control diseases such as mildew when applied directly to plant tissues.

◥ BUY BENEFICIAL BOOSTERS. Another way to increase the micro-organism content of your soil is to buy packaged soil amendments that have been enriched with these beneficial microbes (usually labeled "mycorrhizae").

◥ PILE ON THE MULCH. For years, gardening books from England have exhorted us to double-dig, thoroughly mix amendments into the soil, and generally put the spade and fork to good use. An alternative method, practiced by some gardeners (including Phoebe Noble, whose compost-laden wheelbarrows are shown below), is to simply mulch all your beds and let the material slowly work its way into the ground. The result? Weed suppression, moisture-retentive soil, and healthier plants.

◥ THINK LIKE MOTHER NATURE. If your gardening approach is more philosophical, consider designing your garden on principles of "permaculture." The goal of this system is to create a self-sustaining environment that requires little or no added water, fertilizer, or pesticides. Permaculture techniques include planting vegetables that fix nitrogen into the soil, rotating crops, sheet-mulching (rather than tilling), and designing plant zones that protect or nourish each other.

The Northwest's wet-winter, dry-summer cycle gives it a Mediterranean climate. Thus, where hardiness allows, we can grow many plants from

plants other Mediterranean climates with little or no extra summer watering. This drought-tolerant plant palette increases in importance as our water supplies are taxed.

There is a giant selection of spring-flowering bulbs to choose from, most from the Mediterranean and South Africa. Mediterranean herbs such as lavender, marjoram, oregano, rosemary, and thyme fit this class as well, as do shrubs like rockrose *(Cistus)*, and trees like cork oak *(Quercus suber)*, edible fig *(Ficus carica)*, Italian stone pine *(Pinus pinea)*, and strawberry tree *(Arbutus unedo)*.

Drought-tolerant Western natives include matilija poppy *(Romneya coulteri)*, California fuchsia *(Zauschneria californica)*, and almost any *Agastache*, penstemon, and sage. The best shrubs include wild lilac *(Ceanothus)*, manzanita *(Arctostaphylos)*, western azalea *(Rhododendron occidentale)*, silktassel

(Garrya), and red flowering currant *(Ribes sanguineum).* Among trees, there are plenty of oaks, pines, and a few vine maples to choose from, but native dogwoods suffer much from disease.

The biggest fraction of our mainstream ornamentals are from China, which has been called by some the "Mother of Gardens." But if China is the mother, as a botanical garden's manager once observed, then England is the nanny; plants from China and most other temperate regions made their way into American nurseries after filtering through British breeding programs.

It would take a long time to even read a list of Chinese plants, which include everything from rhododendrons and camellias to hardy palms and bamboos. And it is not as if England didn't have enough to do. They've contributed a host of their own plants, including everything from oaks and yews to bluebells, heathers, primroses, and an impressive array of broad-leafed evergreens, including English ivy, holly, and laurel.

facing page *Drought-tolerant Mediterranean natives like alliums and lavender thrive in a Victoria garden, along with other unthirsty plants.*

influences

In addition to the foreign plants that have shaped Northwest gardens, other immigrants have contributed to Northwest horticulture over the past 150 years—the numerous ethnic groups that arrived in successive waves. You see their wide-reaching influences in Dutch-owned bulb fields in Mt. Vernon, Puyallup, and the Willamette Valley; in Hispanic salsa farms east of the Cascades; in English cottage gardens that dot the urban landscape; and in Russian plants that started showing up in Northwest gardens after the iron curtain came down.

out of asia

Every immigrant group has a compelling story to tell, such as that of the Harui family. A century ago, Zenhichi Harui felt intense economic pressure to leave his farm in Gifu, Japan, and join his brother on Bainbridge Island. But long hours and low wages finally convinced the brothers to leave the mill and start farming berries for the Seattle market. They soon opened a roadside fruit stand, grocery store, gas station, greenhouse, and nursery. They built the elaborate, Japanese-style sunken gardens pictured below, complete with waterfalls and streams; and one day in the 1920s, Zenhichi took two small, flexible pear trees and grafted them into the shape of a giant pear.

Life was good until December 7, 1941. Like many Japanese-American families, the Haruis had to leave everything in the hands of managers and relocate in the interior. After the war, the gardens, greenhouses, and nursery were in ruins. The brothers tried to rebuild, but age and short capital held them back. Decades later, Junkoh and Chris Harui (Zenhichi's son and daughter-in-law) resurrected the old nursery. When they first walked the property, they found a huge stand of Japanese red pines that had rooted through the pots and into the ground. Today, they are the largest in Washington. They also found the grafted pear tree, still living after decades of neglect. If you visit the family's restored gardens today, you can still see the tree in a memorial garden, witness to a horticultural heritage. (Bainbridge Gardens, 9415 Miller Rd. NE, Bainbridge Island, WA 98110 (206) 842-5888/ www.bainbridgegardens.com)

little england

Vancouver and Victoria are generally considered the most British of Canadian cities. Indeed, Victoria, with its double-decker buses, lush hanging baskets, and neighborhoods that lie behind the "Tweed Curtain," is dubbed by some the "Little England of the West." The British influence is reflected in Victoria's carefully designed and well-tended gardens, both private and public. But does this passion for plants represent a copycat similarity to the old country or—worse—a lack of imagination?

Certainly tradition plays a part. "Most of Victoria's original settlers came from the British Isles," says Vancouver-based landscape architect Ron Rule. "And by the turn of the century, there were probably 20 to 30 truly great private gardens in Victoria." Rule is as familiar as anyone with English garden style; he worked for years with consummate English gardener Rosemary Verey at her garden, Barnsley. But English-style gardens were also built in other Canadian cities, such as Toronto—so is there something else to it? According to Rule, what sets Victoria apart is its environment—not just its moderate climate, but also the quality of the light, which makes plants seem to glow even on the grayest days.

Also, much of the Northwest is dominated by conifers—Douglas fir, cedars, and hemlock. "In a garden, they create a very dark, deep-green backdrop that absorbs a lot of light," says Rule. But the Garry oaks and other deciduous trees found on southern Vancouver Island have a less overwhelming presence, casting dappled shade, and creating a softer overall ambience reminiscent of the English countryside.

And, like the English, many residents of British Columbia are devoted to the countryside, so much that the boundary between private and public land tends to blur. Streets are filled with flowers. Public footpaths abound. Pub window boxes overflow with color. Swathes of meadow flow through the parks. With all this bounty, it's not surprising that many gardeners here are so advanced in their knowledge of plants. Rule cites the Wright garden in Vancouver (below) as an example. "The whole family loves to garden," he says. "People here have gardening in their blood." The result is a tremendous range of personal expression— and some pretty extraordinary gardens.

gardens

WATER · WOODLAND · ASIAN
INFLUENCE · NATURAL · MEADOW
MOUNTAIN · ALASKA · COUNTRY
COTTAGE · SANCTUARY · SUBURBIA
TOWN · ROOF TOP · MEDITERRANEAN
TROPICAL · EDIBLE

MUCH IN THE PACIFIC NORTHWEST IS DEFINED BY WATER, BE IT A FERRY COMMUTE, WEEKENDS SPENT SAILING OR PADDLING, OR GARDENING AT THE WATER'S EDGE.

water

Puget Sound is fringed with miles of shoreline where gardeners may have water views, or property that leads to a rocky harbor, dramatic cliffs, or sandy beaches. Graceful sweeps of lawn edged with rhododendrons nudge quiet coves around Lake Washington and Vancouver Island's Saanich Peninsula. Houseboats on Lake Union display pots of flowers and vegetables on their decks. On Whidbey Island and in the San Juans, beachfront vacation cottages, occupied mostly in summer, are decked out with annuals and grasses for quick and plentiful payoff. These summer gardens are often playful places where their owners indulge in fantasy, planting lettuce in an old rowboat, for example, or displaying silky neon windsocks or flags among containers of dazzling marigolds or vibrant geraniums.

If you live where winds are constant, choose tough plants that stand up to strong breezes and salt spray (take cues from what grows there naturally). If your soil is very sandy, build raised beds and fill them with topsoil. Above all, create a garden that celebrates the beauty and power of your coastal or lakeside site.

A wooden board-walk on Pat and Bob Morgan's property zigzags its way to a driftwood arbor overlooking the water. Designed by T.M. Holtschlag, the arbor was built using downed madrone branches piled atop peeled posts. These small, twisted branches mimic the nearby shrubs but don't obstruct the view.

above Although it looks like a naturalistic California garden, this carefully planned hillside planting is on Bowen Island. The drought-tolerant mix includes green lavender *(Lavandula viridis)*, *Artemisia* 'Powis Castle', 'Moonshine' yarrow, *Teucrium fruticans,* and native Pacific Coast iris. {KATHY LEISHMAN GARDEN}

right Kathy Leishman's garden is surrounded by water, yet it regularly experiences summer drought. That doesn't bother these unthirsty grasses and grasslike plants, which include *Calamagrostis × acutiflora* 'Overdam', New Zealand flax 'Yellow Wave', and golden bamboo *(Phyllostachys aurea)*. Grasses are a great choice for coastal gardens, as they hold their upright shape even in the windiest spots.

above Frozen in time, these smooth pebbles were collected on the beach and set in a mortar mix between slatelike pavers.

left A curving stone bank, built by June Granat, faces a Lake Union dock that is berth to ten houseboats and an eye-catching container garden. To celebrate the memory of her mother, daughter Gina Marie Granat acts as steward for the floating flowerfest. She planted the bank with *Canna* 'Tropicanna', dahlias, hardy fuchsias, and evergreens.

below Unusual marine artifacts and a collection of lush containers snuggle into a charming corner on board. Artist Lynda Nielson designed many of the containers, which are filled with coleus, succulents, begonias, jade plant, geraniums, and even a white rose. A dockside greenhouse provides an on-shore winter home for tender plants.

right Gina Marie and her sister, Gayla Field, own the dock. Gina Marie tends a narrow 300-ft-/ 100-m-long planter that they affectionately refer to as "the trough." Gina Marie cares for the ever-changing collection of bright annuals like cosmos, vegetables, and other cheerful plants by putting on her swim suit and diving off the dock. Once in the water, she can deadhead, harvest, and replant to her heart's content.

above This walkway, hung with wisteria, leads from the house to a carport. The path seems to hover over the pond, which is artfully ringed with ferns and horsetail. In the background, a 'Dortmund' rose clambers over the property's original well—Jocelyn Horder likes to leave such traces of the past in place. left When Horder began landscaping her garden, she wanted to leave the view of Liberty Bay intact year-round. So she tucked in moss-covered granite boulders from the Cascades and surrounded them with low-growing evergreens—like dwarf rhododendrons, barberry, and lupines— along with easy perennials such as ox-eye daisy and rudbeckia. {DAN ROBINSON DESIGN}

SEATTLE, WA

on the sound

Some gardeners have fountains, ponds, or streams; Charlene Towne and her husband, Nolan Gimpel, prefer their own "borrowed" water features: lighthouses, sailboats, and ferries. That's why landscape architect Brett Aalderink was careful not to block any sea views when putting together their meadow-style garden. All the plants are low- or medium-height and fairly casual in their growth habits, so they don't require a lot of clipping and pruning. Flowers such as Shasta daisies and crocosmia were chosen for their long blooming periods and for cutting; lavender, grasses, and *Eryngium* are used for dried arrangements.

The result is a colorful tumble of plants placed around small areas of sod, and woven through with pathways. The pinks, purples, and reds that predominate glow even on gray or cloudy days. Light-textured grasses move with the ocean breezes. And, because the garden is carefree and easy to tend, Towne and Gimpel have time to watch the ships sail out to sea.

facing page On a sunny July day, the house, lawn, and walkways are framed by the crisp colors and textures of pink 'Autumn Joy' sedum, *Crocosmia* 'Lucifer', 'Mönch' asters, Mexican feather grass, lavenders, and Shasta daisies. The pathway weaves much like a shoreline.

right Seaside gardeners know how to enjoy their views from indoors or out. The crisp white bed edging and soft-gray–colored decking are vaguely nautical in appearance. Stiff-leafed *Miscanthus sinensis* 'Gracillimus', an artichoke left to flower, and a metal wind sculpture all make interesting silhouettes against the sea and sky.

below Fragrant 'Provence' lavender and 'Stargazer' lily perfume the seating areas on this deck, while loose-textured flowering plants such as asters and bacopa soften the linearity of the decking.

A Northwest woodland garden is mossy, wet, and green. Among the trees, bulbs unfurl pink or blue flowers in spring, and deciduous trees turn brilliant gold and red in fall.

woodland

There's no mistaking a real Northwest woodland. Tall conifers such as Douglas fir or Port Orford cedar create a cathedral of massive trunks and a green canopy that sunlight penetrates only in isolated pools on the forest floor. Beneath the conifers, the lacy leaves of vine maples flutter in the slightest breeze, and ferns edge duff-covered paths.

When creating a woodland garden, look to the forests for inspiration. Position plants to borrow or frame views of surrounding native woodland. Plant in layers—tallest trees in back, mid-sized trees in the center, then billowing shrubs and ground covers toward the front. Mix in dwarf conifers of different shapes and shades of green, and add a few fiery foliaged shrubs. For spring color, try candelabra primroses and miniature daffodils. And don't forget to bring in a mossy rock or two, and a natural-looking pond.

The shift from one bright green texture to another is soft and subtle along this wood-chip path, which is punctuated with pale touches of creamy viburnum and clusters of golden-yellow-flowered *Corydalis lutea*. {JAN WALTEMATH DESIGN}

below A fallen tree makes room for a shaft of sunlight through a shady canopy on Bainbridge Island. Both deciduous and evergreen native ferns and Welsh poppies (Meconopsis cambrica) take advantage of this patch of light.

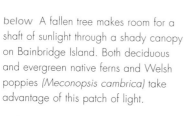

above and left The allure of a woodland garden comes from the cool darkness under tall trees. The path winding through Alan and Shirley Smith's woodland is edged with white-flowered *Erythronium oregonum*, tree heath (*Erica arborea*), and an arch of cream bush (*Holodiscus discolor*). Elsewhere, a grouping of yellow *Ranunculus ficarius* and *Primula japonica*, not yet in bloom, sits at the base of a moss-speckled rocky slope. A large and unseen Garry oak shades the entire area.

right Enveloped by shade-loving plants, a pond makes a
half-hidden focal point in a woodland garden. Shown here
is the lowest of three man-made connecting ponds. It spills as
a waterfall into a stream past pink and red *Primula japonica*,
bright green piggy-back plant *(Tolmiea menziesii)* and bluebells.
To the left are creamy plumes of false Solomon's seal, ferns,
white-puffed sweet woodruff, and more pink and red primulas.

left Back in 1960, Juki
Lida, along with five other
garden designers, installed
the stones and plantings
for this wooded stream in
the Japanese Garden at
Seattle's Washington
Park Arboretum. Mature
Japanese maples provide
the bright green treetop
cover, with pink rhodo-
dendrons peeking through
the canopy. Evergreen
azaleas, lady ferns, and
sword ferns follow the
curves of the large mossy
boulders that were
brought in from the
Cascade Range.

above A gnarled mossy stump, so emblematic of the Northwest, reminds us that the forest—and our gardens—are a blend of change, age, and continuity.

left Phyllis and Richard Null, the owners of this peacefully wooded Eugene garden, used a Washington stone called "windswept moss rock" to create a pond near some old fruiting cherry trees. They mixed red 'Halcro' tulips and yellow daffodils (*Cyclamineus* hybrid) with forget-me-nots and blue-bells. The red leaves of *Photinia × fraseri*, and sharp greens of scotch moss, *Nandina domestica*, and euphorbia add to the early spring show.

THIS GARDEN IS FILLED NOT ONLY WITH THE COLORS AND CONTRASTS
OF THE FOREST, BUT ALSO WITH ITS SOUNDS, SMELLS, AND TEXTURES.

BAINBRIDGE ISLAND, WA

in the woods

Bobbie Garthwaite and Joe Sullivan loved this natural, wooded property when they purchased it back in 1990. But the grounds had been neglected for some time and so the work began. They excavated silt-filled water features, rebuilt bridges, and sifted through rhododendrons that had taken over.

Garthwaite says the garden is tidiest near the water because that is where she and Sullivan like to spend time, drawn to the sound of water moving through their network of streams, ponds, and waterfalls. It roars during the rainy winter, changing to a soft murmur during the drier months of summer.

The couple likes to wander their woodland garden barefoot, savoring the mosses and other soft ground covers, like jewel mint of Corsica *(Mentha requienii)*, releasing fragrance with each step. The sounds of birds, and wind in the trees, complete this woodland garden.

facing page A natural spring-fed stream continuously fills and empties three ponds and three waterfalls in the one and a half-acre garden. Sullivan made the path for the lush, shade-loving ferns, creamy white *Smilacina racemosa, Primula japonica, Tolmiea menziesii,* and delicate white-flowered *Galium odoratum* surrounding this pond. Other waterside plants found in the garden include iris, *Myosotis scorpioides,* and *Primula pulverulenta* 'Bartley,' as seen here in the oval frame.

above A shallow-sided concrete chute, filled with soil and mosses, crosses the stream. Sullivan molded the stepping-stones that mark the way over the bridge with designs representing the sun, the wind, shells, and leaves. Native moss, *Primula japonica,* crocus, *Sagina subulata,* and *Tolmiea menziesii* harmonize in this tree-shaded area. {LITTLE AND LEWIS DESIGN}

right Apple-green rosettes of *Primula japonica* embellish a sea of mixed mosses, and drifts of pink and blue forget-me-nots rise like islands above and below. The couple use many other ground-hugging plants, like violets, wild cyclamen, *Veronica repens,* and *Lysimachia nummularia.*

TRADITIONAL TECHNIQUES AND MATERIALS FROM CHINA, JAPAN, KOREA (AND INCREASINGLY, INDONESIA AND THAILAND) ARE LOVINGLY INTEGRATED INTO MANY NORTHWEST GARDENS.

asian influence

What is an Asian garden? Is it a pristine bed of raked gravel and boulders that mimic the oceanic islands of Japan? Or is it a splash of maple foliage surrounding a pond sparkling with koi? Perhaps a pathway through a stand of black bamboo leading to a handcrafted tea house? Or is a "real" Asian garden a naturalistic forest glade filled with gnarled pines and contorted bonsai?

Any of these elements can be found in a true Asian garden. It may be thanks to a third-generation Japanese-American gardener who wishes to honor her ancestors in an outdoor Buddhist shrine, or because a builder is attracted to the strength and longevity of bamboo fencing. Gardeners may draw inspiration from our scenery—mountains, rocks, water, and woods—which is similar to that of Central and coastal Asia. But one thing is certain: the influences of the "East" (which lies to our west) are brushed through our gardens like strokes of calligraphy in an ancient scroll.

left Part artistry and part architecture, this gazebo and the bell it houses feel like a woodland shrine in a Kenmore, WA garden. A path of stone pavers leads to the structure, where visitors can rest in contemplation, or break the silence with a gong that recalls an ancient temple {ILGA JANSONS/MIKE DRYFOOS GARDEN}

below A maple turns fiery orange in fall, complementing the bamboo fence known as Misu Gaki style.

facing page Stone steps lead to a grove of vine maples. The trees' slender trucks rise gracefully in a moist, naturally wooded area.

right Asian-style gardens tucked into the Northwest woods create classic landscapes by any cultural definition. This garden depends on a gentle slope to create an amphitheater-like display for rocks, water, and plants. As the water drips and splashes downward, it adds to the experience.
{ILGA JANSONS/MIKE DRYFOOS GARDEN}

THROUGH THE EYES OF AN ARTIST WHO WORKS IN THREE DIMENSIONS, A
GARDEN PLAYS UP SHAPE, STRUCTURE, DETAIL, AND TRANSITION.

METCHOSIN, B.C.

stroll garden

When Robin Hopper invites you to take a stroll in the garden, he is not talking about a dignified turn past clipped hedges as in his native England. Rather, this ceramicist, author, teacher, and former travel guide is referring to a personal journey through a series of linked spaces that together form a garden covering three acres.

The scale of Hopper's garden is impressive, yet never obtrusive. The overall shape is that of two concentric circles. The outer circle is an ever-changing pathway that leads through woods, meadows, a "gladiator" tunnel, a bamboo grove, and a bog garden dedicated to the memory of a dear friend. The inner circle is a private, walled meditation courtyard and two-tiered pond, visible from many vantage points throughout Hopper's house.

Everywhere you are struck by the attention to detail, from the lashed bamboo latches on the gates to the sculptures in all media and sizes. Truly a work of art, this garden.

facing page The inner courtyard is designed for contemplation and observation as light and shadow change through the day. Birds dip and soar constantly, drawn by the pond and fountains.

above There are many windows in the studios, showroom, and home of Hopper and his wife, fellow-potter Judi Dyelle. One of his favorite views is from the kitchen sink, where he can watch Japanese maples illuminate the fall garden, including clockwise from top left *Acer palmatum* 'Filigree', *A.p.* 'Osakazuki', *A.p.* 'Dissectum Garnet', and *A.p.* 'Murasaki Kiyo hime'.

left From a bright-red "Bridge Over the River Koi" you look down on a paved surface inlaid with handmade pebbles and Hopper's ceramic goldfish, which gradually blend into a green ocean of lawn. Most of the 100 fish are headed downstream; but there are eight who gamely refuse to go with the flow, much like the gardener himself (both numbers are propitious in Chinese numerology).

"NATURALLY NORTHWEST" GARDENS CELEBRATE OUR NATIVE LANDSCAPES IN ALL THEIR GORGEOUS SHADES AND SUBTLETIES.

natural

A natural-looking garden blends together elements that seem to have been lifted from our majestic wild landscape—but it does so with a light touch. In wooded areas, shrubs and trees are shown up against the native timber beyond the garden's boundaries—a concept that the Japanese call "shakkei," or borrowed scenery. Moss-encrusted boulders anchor the garden plantings, and form stony piles that resemble ancient glacial deposits. Ground covers sweep across the earth, and ferns dangle beside ponds. In pastoral valleys, grasses mingle with seasonal bulbs and wild-flowers around fences and sheds of weath-ered wood.

Natural gardens make the most of what the land provides, whether shades of green, or frost-browned grasses, or twisted, leafless trees that form striking silhouettes against winter-gray skies. They echo the plants found on Northwest rambles, whether rhododendrons, wildflowers, beach grass, or maples flaming like bonfires in the shade of Douglas firs.

above, left A stand of spring-blooming native camass flows like a mountain stream through this meadow garden.

above, right Twenty years ago, Glen Patterson chose this North Vancouver property not for its English-style garden, but for its rocky outcroppings, Douglas firs, and views across the water to Lighthouse Park. Now the lawns and hybrid teas are long gone, replaced with a garden inspired by visits to Japan and the help of designer Jim Nakano. It's filled with time-scarred boulders, winding pebbled paths, ponds, and perhaps most important—open spaces that Patterson calls "places for the spirit."

above The plants in Glen Patterson's garden reflect a sense of place. Japanese maples, evergreen conifers, and species rhododendrons are pruned in an "open-cloud" way so that their branch structure can be appreciated. Around these larger plants, ferns, candelabra primroses, and small-leafed, low-growing shrubs pocket the ground.

below Many Northwest properties contain boggy areas, streams, ponds, or vernal pools; the best man-made water features reflect nature's own designs. In the Kraus garden in Ryderwood, Washington, the pool was lined, and then covered with river rock and surrounded with boulders. The water circulates through the pond's two levels. The grasses in the pond include Columbia sedge (Carex obnupta) and beige miniature cattails (Typha minima). {EAMONN HUGHES DESIGN}

A PASSION FOR THE ART OF BONSAI AND A DEEP LOVE FOR THE HIGH CASCADES COMBINE TO CREATE A GARDEN THAT ECHOES THE PAST BUT LIVES IN THE PRESENT.

elandan

Naturalistic gardens encourage us to sharpen our powers of observation. The intricate root system of a long-uprooted stump, the depth and shadow of a grove of trees, the myriad colors in a pebbled pathway, a miniature map of moss traced on an ancient boulder—these small details contain within them reflections of the larger landscape around us. Dan Robinson understands this, and his six-acre ocean-front garden reflects it.

Robinson created the garden in order to house his bonsai collection, but the garden has become a desti-nation in itself. As he says, "Everything is sculptural." Winding pathways lead the visitor's eye up to an impos-ing snag set starkly against the sky, or out over the water, or down to a crevice in an ancient boulder deco-rated with a fractal pattern of lichen. The overall effect is peaceful yet powerful, much like the Northwest landscape that inspired it.

Elandan lies in a sheltered saltwater inlet on Puget Sound. Dan and his son, William, brought in thousands of tons of dirt and over 800 tons of granite boulders to the site. In less than 10 years, the garden has developed an ambience of age, due to the presence of ancient specimens, such as this 3,000-year-old juniper snag.

left Among the treasured bonsai specimens in Robinson's garden are this evergreen Kurumi azalea, which dates back to 1840.

below Stumps, snags, and the weathered spires of surf-bleached trees have become integral elements in this garden. Here, a penstemon seems to grow out of a boulder, while a small-leafed azalea and epimedium creep around the base of an 800-year-old Ponderosa pine.

homegrown

Our Northwest native plants have traveled far from home. From *Lewisias* to columbines, ceanothus to kinnikinnick, they have taken up residence in European gardens whose owners know a good thing when they see it.

Increasingly, so do we. Art and Mareen Kruckeberg, founding members of the Washington Native Plant Society, get much of the credit for that. Art, the botanist, writes and teaches at the University of Washington; while Mareen, the horticulturist, runs MsK Nursery in Seattle (20066 15th Ave. NW, Shoreline, WA 98177; 206-546-1281).

"I sell a few exotic plants too, like wood anemone," says Mareen, "but lots of customers walk straight past them to the native section." That's no surprise to anybody who has visited the four-acre garden and seen how effective natives are in the landscape, or read Art's classic book, *Gardening With Native Plants of the Pacific Northwest*.

Since Mareen founded her nursery, she's sold scores of tanoak, Garry oak, Oregon grape, *Philadelphus*, vine maple, *Garrya*, and red-flowering currant. Some she starts from seed, and others she digs out of the forest duff on her property. Among woodland plants, she recommends *Vancouverias*, Oregon oxalis, and *Maianthemum* because they're so easy. Then there are the deer ferns, wild ginger, maidenhair ferns, and trilliums . . . a nearly endless list of plants.

Art has his favorites too: fawn lilies, vanilla leaf, *Lewisia tweedyi*, mountain hemlock, Douglas and vine maple, manzanita, and serviceberry. He leads field trips to these plants in the wild, then encourages his pupils to study them. Together, the Kruckebergs continue to remind us of the wealth of plants that grow all around us.

FLOWERS, SUNSHINE, AND TALL SUMMER GRASS BECKON US TO LIE ON
OUR BACKS, LOOK FOR SHAPES IN THE CLOUDS, AND LISTEN TO THE SOFT
HUM OF BEES.

meadow

It's tempting to think that meadow gardens are a modern idea, but native Northwest gardeners used fire to make them for centuries. They did it mostly as a way of managing for native camass, an edible bulb. But is it far-fetched to imagine that they, too, were lying on their backs looking into the sky?

Today's meadows are mostly blends of naturalized grasses and flowers that you mow three or four times a summer, weed occasionally, and enjoy constantly. But like any combination of garden plants, they prosper with soil preparation, watering, and fertilization. If you don't quite have the nerve to convert your lawn to a meadow at once, try this: Rough it up with a thatch rake, scatter some viola and English daisy seeds over it, and set your mower to cut a little higher. Before you know it, you'll have the beginnings of a meadow.

Robin Hopper's British Columbia meadow is filled with a combination of coastal wildflowers, perennials, and non-native grasses. The mix includes California poppies, coreopsis, Mexican feather grass, gaillardia, and bachelor's buttons. Spring- and summer-flowering bulbs include *Allium cernuum*, *A. karataviense*, and *Nectaroscordum siculum*.

above Except for the modern home on this coastal property, the land is little changed since well before English bedding schemes arrived on Vancouver Island. The flowers of purple camass (Camassia quamash) and red flowering currant (Ribes sanguineum) cloak the mossy meadow with color in the spring. Rocky outcroppings provide natural garden sculpture. {CAMPBELL GARDEN}

left Backed by Douglas firs, this high alpine meadow in Washington flowers for a brief but brilliant period in spring.

below Northwest natives such as lupines will happily naturalize in a meadow planting; these are accompanied by sun-loving euphorbias.

IN THE CRYSTALLINE AIR OF THE NORTHWEST MOUNTAINS, GARDENERS FEEL THEY'VE NEVER SEEN KENTUCKY BLUEGRASS SO GREEN, SHASTA DAISIES SO WHITE, OR LILIES SO FAIR.

mountain

New arrivals often come to the mountains thinking in terms of trade: They're willing to give up much of the low-elevation plant palette in exchange for real seasons, pure air, and stunning vistas. But they soon realize that they'll never exhaust the list of cold-climate plants, to say nothing of the stunning plant combinations that are possible in high mountains.

Aspen leaves flicker in the lightest breeze, turning butter-yellow in fall. Penstemons and other alpine plants run riot, and fresh snow cloaks native conifers.

Mountain soils tend to be thin, but that allows boulders to become landscaping elements. Raised beds surrounded by gathered stones are beautiful, and in worst cases, they may present the best planting option. Sloping topography sets up opportunities for cascades and waterfalls that can look unnatural down below. It's a different world up high, and few mountain gardeners would trade it.

This Montana property was once a working ranch, but the fences have since come down and the cattle have moved on. Now, an irregular stone path filled in with bright green *Sagina subulata* not only borders a planting area, but draws the eye quite naturally to the hills and trees beyond.

above Lourdes and Rick Dempster have planted thousands of trees, shrubs, and annuals in their 3-acre, Kelowna, B.C. garden. This grouping includes junipers, a weeping cypress, pink tamarisk, several pines, and *Viburnum opulus*.

left To brighten up the dark green background of cottonwoods, pines, and aspens, Judy Whitmyre filled her garden with the fair blooms of bearded iris, ox-eye daisies, columbines, and 'Johnson's Blue' geraniums. Drifts of lupine echo the sloping lines of the Pioneer Mountains, which form a distant backdrop for this Idaho garden.

facing page Patches of lupines, chives, columbines, painted daisies, Oriental poppies, lady's mantle, dianthus, and bearded iris fill Judy Whitmyre's Sun Valley mountain garden. How does she keep the deer away? "I use blood meal," says Whitmyre. "They don't like the scent. I start early in the season and sprinkle a small amount in and around the garden every three days. Works like a charm!"

left Space isn't tight in the Dempsters' garden. The first task when they moved to the property was to clear the existing vegetation and start over. The garden now contains ponds, streams, a swimming pool, two gazebos, and many different smaller gardens intricately cut through with meandering pathways. After turning the corner into this conifer grove, you find yourself face-to-face with a lovely abundance of *Lilium* 'Pink Sorbet'.

A REMOTE MOUNTAIN GARDEN BURSTS INTO
COLOR FOR A SHORT BUT WONDERFUL SUMMER.

ATLIN, B.C.

cabin fever

Gardeners living in the historic gold
mining town of Atlin in far northern
B.C. have a limited season in which to
garden, so they make the most of it.
And so it is with Catherine Regehr,
the owner of this picturesque property.

She arrives at her log home at the
end of May and begins by feeding
all the plants with a hefty 18-18-18
fertilizer, pruning lilacs, replacing
delphiniums lost to frost, and dividing
poppies. Rhubarb does well in Atlin's
clay-based, nutrient-poor soil, so
Regehr cultivates more than 100
plants as a large-leafed groundcover.

She shares the land with ospreys,
foxes, and an occasional bear family,
but says she isn't fond of moose that
eat the lilacs! Her greatest joy comes
from painting in her studio while
looking out at the blooming garden
and the snow-capped mountains
framing the Juneau ice field.

above and right Bright Icelandic
poppies (above) and yarrow (on the right)
capture the essence of long sunlit summer
days and nights up north, only 60 miles/
100 kilometers from the Yukon. Intense
purple and dark-blue giant delphiniums
('Galahad' and 'Arthur', respectively)
reflect the cool background undertones
of Atlin Lake and Atlin Mountain.

Masses of delphiniums,
poppies, columbines, tiger
lilies, Siberian iris, veronicas,
and lupines swirl around the
log home, traveling from
the upper stone steps into
a lower planting contained
by a stone wall. The seeds
for the Shirley poppy (below)
were collected at a nearby
mineral-spring well. And the
log home, patterned after
an old *Goldrush* roadhouse,
was designed and built
by Regehr herself.

THANK GOODNESS FOR WINTER: IT'S TIME TO DEVELOP STRATEGIES, DESIGN
BORDERS, ORDER PLANTS, AND GET READY TO SQUEEZE THE MOST OUT OF THE
NEXT WONDERFUL SUMMER.

Alaska

Gardening in Alaska is, like everything else here, BIG. Brobdingnagian cabbages spring up during 19-hour days in the fertile Matanuska Valley; rain forests make dripping shade gardens a major focus in the Southeastern part of the state; and the passion for gardening emerges triumphant after months of cold and dark.

The problems are supersized as well. Winter delivers serious cold that heaves soil and tests the limits of the hardiest plants. Lumbering moose displace deer as the garden's most serious four-legged predators.

Gardeners are more than equal to the challenges, however, getting the jump on spring with greenhouses and cold frames; warming the soil with high-tech infrared-transmitting (IRT) mulches; and extending the season with row covers. They're constantly testing too. It happens on the university level at Georgeson Botanical Garden, where ongoing trials spotlight the best plants for the climate; and on the individual level, where gardeners methodically try every peony, or every species rose, to learn which plants are tough enough to brighten their gardens come summer.

Annuals are popular up north, and for good reason. They quickly grow tall enough to screen areas under decks or around eyesores. In this garden in Homer, a foreground mixture of pink and white cosmos, marigolds, and lobelia segues into a blend of rosy-hued poppies. To tie together the deck and the garden, the designer filled oak barrels with similar colors.

left To encourage this patch of red and violet annual poppies to self-sow, Les Brake tears them out in September and top-dresses the bed with sterilized manure. Thanks to this helping hand, the poppies re-emerge each season to accompany double pink peonies and purple *Campanula lactifolia.*

below A clump of pink dianthus anchors the corner of a perennial bed whose center-piece of tall delphiniums masks the grade change between two sections of lawn. The rocks outlining the bed echo the hues of stones set loosely in stair-steps.

above Fragrant wood smoke, a warm fire, and rustic furniture bring a sensual warmth to this garden on long, cool evenings. Flame-colored flowers jostle for space in the perennial borders, crowded between packed-earth pathways that separate the cool lawn from the hot flower beds.

right True to their name, each daylily bloom lasts just 24 hours, but that's a long time in the land of the midnight sun. In this northern garden, they mingle with white astilbe.

above Much like a raised bed, a window box gives flowering plants perfect soil, good exposure, and a protected spot out of reach of nibbling elk and curious children. This one on an Anchorage log cabin is filled with red geraniums and blue lobelia.
{GOODWIN ARANT GARDEN}

right This bent-alder porch railing crafted by Jerry Conrad offers a see-through view of a classic cottage garden. Peonies are blooming now, entwined with 'Johnson's Blue' geraniums. A soft magenta haze of *Dianthus deltoides* fills in the space below the porch.

against the odds

The first time you visit Alaska, its grandeur will steal your heart. Hot-pink fireweed carpets its meadows. Glaciers sparkle like blue crystal between knife-edged peaks. And white water roars through rocky gorges, sending up clouds of mist. Even the gardens are grand; in them, flowers, vegetables, and berries grew lush and rampant, and sumptuous fuchsias and tuberous begonias dangle from hanging baskets. This is short-season gardening at its best.

Sure, this lovely land presents challenges. Moose graze on lawns and lettuce. Grizzlies break fruit trees in half. The soil never warms much above above 60°F/15°C. And during the long winters, bone-chilling subzero temperatures freeze everything in sight, while heavy snows snap tree branches.

"My Alaskan friends laugh off these inconveniences," says Kathy Brenzel, who has come to love this northern land. "We sit on their decks outside Anchorage watching Dall sheep graze high on the cliffs across the valley, and rabbits sniffing out the peas in the vegetable patch."

What's inspiring about her friends, says Brenzel, is their zest for gardening. "They know that, up here, you need ingenuity and a can-do attitude to grow plants well. But the rewards for your efforts are sweet."

She's right. When summer brings 20 hours a day of sunlight, it's pay-back time. Rhubarb grows lush and large. Delphiniums tickle house eaves. And cabbages reach mammoth proportions. How do Alaskans make this happen?

❧ GROW HIGHER. Gently mound soil, or put it in raised beds. It will warm up more quickly in spring than level ground.

❧ MULCH PLANTINGS. Cover planting beds with infrared-transmitting plastic sheeting. Cut slits through the plastic and plant seedlings through them. For added heat, fill clear plastic beverage bottles with tea and place them on the plastic cover over the plants' root zones. The dark liquid absorbs the solar heat during the day and releases it at night.

❧ USE ROW COVERS. If spring and summer are chilly, cover the bed with a lightweight fabric that transmits light but holds in heat.

❧ CONTAIN HEAT-LOVERS. Crops such as peppers and tomatoes (especially Sweet 100s) thrive in 5-gallon cans of soil. Keep them in a warm greenhouse or solarium.

❧ CHOOSE WELL. Varieties with a proven track record help guarantee the best harvest. Some favorites with Alaskans: 'Earlivee' yellow sweet corn, 'Nantes' carrots, 'Ithaca' and 'Salinas' lettuce, and 'Golden Hubbard' squash.

❧ ADD WINTER INTEREST. A border of low-growing conifers such as dwarf mugho pine can give structure to garden beds in winter when everything else is dormant, and is especially pretty when dusted with snow. In summer, the conifer foliage provides a rich green backdrop for flowers such as forget-me-nots, johnny jump-ups, nemesias, violas, and yarrow. (After all, why not show off the flowers, which blaze more brilliantly here where the sun arcs lower in the sky than "outside.")

COUNTRY GARDENERS TAKE MORE TIME THAN THEIR CITY COUNTERPARTS,
HAVE MORE QUIET, AND FEEL MORE CONNECTED WITH THE LOCAL PLANTS
JUST OVER THE FENCE. THAT'S WHY THEY CAME TO
THE COUNTRY TO BEGIN WITH.

country

Gardens outside the limits of cities and suburbs are usually
rambling blends of old-fashioned flowers and vegetables. They're nour-
ished by a compost pile hidden behind the toolshed, and surrounded
by a rustic wattle fence that is so becoming you hardly realize why it is
there: to keep out the deer.

The country presents us with a multitude of small but momentous
events, which gardeners soon come to know. Not long after the pussy
willows are ready to cut, spring's first frog songs ring out and the year's
first mosquito bite is felt. A month later swallows careen overhead,
trilliums carpet the forest floor, and dogwoods light up the edges of the
woodland. As the corn rises up to find the summer sun, the bats come
back, and when the bats leave, the corn is ready to pick.

Country gardeners know these things, and are changed by them. It's
life by rhythm, not by calendar.

Cobalt-blue gazing balls look like hot-air balloons waiting to rise up into the sky over Geoff
Beasley's garden. Surrounded by spears of purple- and lavender-colored delphiniums, the
balls reflect the barn, the clouds, and the surrounding trees.

below Big, boisterous country plants include sunflowers, spider flower, and larkspur. These grow happily in a Lopez Island farm because the entire property is encircled with a fence that keeps out foraging animals, both wild and domestic. {LANGENBACH GARDEN}

above Fog clings like smoke to the surface of the duck pond at Red Gate Farm, an example of the serenity of a country garden. The wooded area houses native trees and a few introduced species, such as paper birch and willow, while the pond is filled with scarlet *Lobelia cardinalis*, irises, and cattails.

left Hollyhock Farm, on Cortes Island, British Columbia, has a teaching garden as well as a kitchen garden that mixes ornamentals and edibles. To brighten the entry, yarrow and poppies are planted at the end of rows of vegetables. A fence and driftwood gate keep the deer from sampling the wares.

left In Geoff Beasley's garden
just outside Portland, a grassy
path beckons visitors to a pasture
gate composed of deep-blue,
symmetrical squares. Artful though
it is, the gate serves as a practical
barrier to keep horses, and other
livestock, in the field. {MICHAEL
SCHMIDT DESIGN}

below Roses and clematis are
a quintessential country and
cottage-garden combination. Here
a 'Lucetta' rose and deciduous
Clematis × *jackmanii* intertwine
up a trellis against a garden
shed. In the foreground are easy
perennials including yarrow,
spiky *Echinops bannaticus*, and
delphiniums, kept in bounds
by low boxwood hedges.

left and above Des and Sandy Kennedy know that gardens reflect their owners. What then to make of a garden filled with old boots and painted oil drums, and scattered about with powder-blue baskets? Whimsy is welcome in a country setting; there's no call for formality. Feel free to recycle old objects and sprinkle touches of humor throughout.

above Country gardeners who don't have ready access to super-sized building centers may have to 'make do' when installing hardscape. All the materials used in this Port Orchard country vegetable garden have been recycled. The stones, fencing, and birdhouse supplies were cast-offs from other gardens. The fence looks a bit rickety, but it serves to keep out the deer—that's why the vegetables and herbs are growing so happily.

left A relaxed and slightly untidy scene greets visitors to Hollyhock Farm. A less-than-vertical, weather-worn gate is overgrown with a wildly asymmetrical collection of violet delphiniums, a climbing rose, and creamy verbascum.

facing page Local sandstone pavers, filled in and around with creeping thyme and lamb's ears, lead up to the front door of Des Kennedy's country home. Picking up on the blue-and-burgundy house colors are a purple clematis and a strawberry pot filled with *Sempervivum tectorum*.

some years ago,

Steve Lorton and his wife, Anna Lou, purchased 10 acres of land near the village of Birdsview in the Skagit River Valley. There they built a house with meadow on three sides and stands of alders and conifers on the fourth. That's where they spend their free days, just an hour's drive from Seattle, surrounded by kids who joyously splash in the pond and run through the woods.

Then came the garden. Lorton started by cultivating and planting around the house, then gradually moving outward to cover 3 acres. Now he says, "If I'm not working in my country garden, I'm thinking about it."

He mowed irregular islands out of the native grasses and planted them with sword ferns and vine maples to echo those growing wild nearby. Then he added perennials, chosen as much for their foliage as for their bloom, including astilbe, bugbane, columbines, daylilies, euphorbia, filipendula, geraniums, meadow rue, peonies, and, in the wooded areas, hellebores by the hundreds.

He planted trees in groves to block, frame, or give depth to views—including glorious vistas of the Cascades. Where the garden blends into the wild land, he planted small trees and shrubs that flower, and others that offer autumn color. He set out bulbs like daffodils and camass, which have naturalized with gusto. As his foray into "Tarzan gardening" deepened, he planted a *Clematis montana* 'Grandiflora' near an ancient cedar. It now crawls high and mightily through the tree, and when cloaked with white blossoms in spring, it looks as though it's covered with roosting doves.

As Lorton says, "I once complained that there was nothing worse than slugs. God was listening, I know, and sent me wild blackberries." But no matter the challenges, he feels a deep and abiding love for his country garden. "It make me hope for reincarnation," he says wistfully, "I want to come back, several times at least, as a bird to nest in my favorite trees!"

THE BEAUTY OF A COTTAGE GARDEN LIES IN ITS CASUAL ELEGANCE, ITS PROFUSION OF BLOOMS, AND ITS JOYFUL EXUBERANCE.

cottage

A cottage garden is usually small, perhaps surrounding a Northwest bungalow. It may have a picket or bent-willow fence, pillowy cabbage roses, or tall stands of hollyhocks or delphiniums. The garden is filled with delightful touches: a gracious birdhouse or birdbath, for instance, a timeless sundial, or an unexpected but treasured sculpture of rusted iron peeking up behind a gaggle of plants. Comfort is key, with Adirondack chairs or a twiggy bench placed to take advantage of pretty views.

There's a look of casual abundance in a cottage garden, with lettuce and veggies growing among flowers, or vines-drenched trellises beside billowing shrubs. Fragrance wafts from old-fashioned favorites like wisteria, lilac, or antique roses. Above all, a cottage garden has a quality of nostalgia that reminds us of quieter, simpler times.

When Pamela and Paul Panum designed their family get-away and its adjacent guesthouse, they carefully chose plants for the garden that would complement the cottage-style architecture. Scrambling over the portico is an 'Honor' climbing rose, and at the base of each pillar are more roses and hydrangeas. Atop it all, a window box is filled with ivy and annual favorites like petunias, lobelia, alyssum, and geraniums.

right Plants meander here and there throughout the Panums' garden, filling in around the house and clambering up the walls and trellises. Here white climbing roses, purple wisteria, and clematis cover the arbor. In the shady area next to the walkway, dwarf boxwood (*Buxus sempervirens* 'Suffruticosa'), hostas, and ferns lead to a pink rhododendron, its color chosen to complement the rosy brickwork.

below Tucked into the nooks and crannies of a cottage garden are charming and personal touches. Here, a handsome cherub dips his toes into a birdbath, surrounded by a protective canopy of 'Forest Pansy' redbud.

left The gray shingles of this remodeled vintage cottage in Neskowin, Oregon, make a cool background for a display of colorful flowers. The dazzling jumble includes snapdragons, white Shasta daisies, nasturtiums, morning glories, delphiniums, California poppies, and bachelor's buttons. To further brighten the house, the owners painted the front door cobalt blue and then topped it with a cheerful awning.

right and below This whimsical cottage sits on 10 acres of pasture, orchard, woods, and wetland. Designed by Holly Turner and Ralph Hastings, Froggwell's borders are filled with pastel-colored flowers (such as the yellow hollyhocks below) and an abundance of green, blue, and burgundy plants chosen for their ability to shine despite frequently gray Whidbey Island skies. A Lady Banks' rose almost smothers the roof, and pathways of grass flow around and between the beds, providing visual foils for the abundant plantings.

heritage gardens

Back when pioneering families were settling the Pacific Northwest, they built charming wood-framed houses in places like Seattle's Queen Anne Hill, along Grand and Rucker avenues in Everett, and in Portland Heights. Architectural styles varied. There were classic Victorians with gingerbread filigree edging their roofs, and beveled-glass windows in the door. Dutch colonials sported turrets and high, square roof peaks. Clapboard cottages were fronted by deep porches meant for sitting. And around these houses the owners planted rambling roses, fruit trees, and hollyhocks. My grandparents began their married life in one of these early-20th-century charmers, and my mother spent her childhood in another not far away in the "historic district" of Everett (near the house shown at right). Both houses are still there. Now, in neighborhoods throughout the Northwest, new homeowners are lovingly restoring these venerable structures, giving them fresh paint, renewed details, and romantic gardens.

I've seen a pale lavender cottage with spikes of mauve hollyhock rising in the front yard, behind a lavender picket fence. Another house is painted robin's-egg blue, and surrounded with pink rambling roses. Bold orange cannas bloom against a gray house with orange trim. In all cases, the flower colors echo or play off the house colors. These gardens inspire us to create romantic, nostalgic gardens of our own.

These gardens inspire us to create romantic, nostalgic gardens of our own; here are a few tips to get started.

❧ BILLOW OUT. Plant shrubs and perennials that put out clouds of fine-textured foliage or have open, graceful growth habits. The voluminous spring flower display of weigela, for instance, makes a glorious accent beside a white wooden gate. Or try baby's breath to soften the spaces between tree roses.

❧ DRIP VINES. Let them clamber and drape over fences, trellises, and house eaves. Plant a *Clematis montana* against a weathered wood fence, or train a wisteria to grow up and over a bold trellis beside a brown-shingled garage.

❧ ADD SPICE. Fragrance evokes the magic of grandmother's garden, so plant perfumemakers like lavender, honeysuckle, lilac, mock orange, and old roses near the front walk or beside a patio.

—KATHLEEN BRENZEL

IN A WORLD THAT OFTEN WHIRLS TOO RAPIDLY AROUND US, OUR GARDENS ARE AMONG THE FEW PLACES WHERE WE FIND PEACE AND TRANQUILITY.

sanctuary

For those in small urban or suburban spaces, the entire garden becomes a sanctuary when surrounded with tall trees and climbing vines that give it privacy from neighboring houses. Or a smaller part of the garden—a corner tucked away from hubs of activity like dining terraces, firepits, or play areas—can be a sanctuary when enclosed with a billowing curtain, a rose-covered trellis, or a screen of woven bamboo.

Whether your sanctuary is an elaborate structure or a simple grouping of furniture, orient it to face a favorite view of water or mountains, or to capture a sunrise or sunset. Then make the space your own. Furnish it for comfort, with cushions, and perhaps lanterns or candles for soft evening light. Bring in pots of fragrant flowers—cottage pinks or stock, for example—or a tinkling tabletop fountain for a little water music. Then relax, and allow nature to unfurl its magic around you.

left An aerie perched high above the garden, this hexagonal tree house fits snugly within the five trunks of an old big-leaf maple. Built against a steep hillside in Tom Speer's woodland garden in Burien, WA, the structure can only be reached by a cantilevered bridge, increasing the sense of privacy.

below What better place than an open-air bedroom to linger over a good book while the birds sing you to sleep? This one is proof that outdoor rooms don't have to be rustic, but can offer a different kind of luxury. It's a spring-through-fall outdoor room, replete with comfortable mattress, bedding, and lampshades, and surrounded by a forest garden of dogwoods, ferns, and astilbe. {FEENEY GARDEN}

facing page Complete with beaver-chewed crossbars, the frame of this daybed was carefully constructed of poles and sturdy sticks collected by its builder, Jeffrey Bale. He tucked the daybed into his hidden back garden in Portland, then hung it with temple bells, and surrounded it with long-flowering perennials such as *Lavatera thuringiaca* 'Barnsley' and *Macleaya microcarpa* 'Summer Haze'. A pathway of mosaic pebbles leads to the bed and a 'Glenora' grape trails along the top crossbar. With a beautiful fabric throw and plenty of cushions, the bed becomes a tranquil retreat for napping or contemplation.

right and below This "machiai," or waiting-bench area, can serve either as a tea house or as a place of solitude to observe the meditation garden of Robin Hopper and Judi Dyelle. The early afternoon sun enters through a carefully placed window, suffusing the machiai with an appropriately mellow spiritual light.

THE SUBURBAN BACKYARD IS USUALLY THE MOST LIVED-IN PART OF THE GARDEN:
PATIOS, DECKS, POOLS, HOT TUBS, AND FIRE PITS MAKE IT INVITING, BUT IT'S STYLE
THAT GIVES EACH GARDEN ITS FLAVOR.

suburbia

Just as most people have a public and a private side, suburban gardens have the same: a front garden—a "gift to the street," as somebody once observed—that greets you when you arrive home; and a rear garden, widely known as the backyard.

Suburban garden design might revolve around a vegetable garden, a few old orchard trees, a children's play yard, or an outdoor eating area. These days many Northwest gardeners are also interested in bringing nature back into the suburbs; where thirsty lawns once stood, backyard wildlife habitats have come into vogue. Mix up trees, groundcovers, and shrubs, and you can have any kind of garden you want. Choose well, and you can have something that wild creatures can use too.

facing page Valerie Murray's home is in a neighborhood blessed with mature oak trees. Murray has taken advantage of every possible nook and cranny in her half-acre lot to create different garden rooms. This intimate backyard leads to a small patio beside the house. Beyond the Japanese maples lies a gazebo, and behind the lawn is a small but thickly planted woodland area.

above Gail Severn's Ketchum home is one of four that share several acres of common area. Clematis and roses ('Agnes', 'Topaz'; and 'William Baffin') tumble around and over the sides of her deck and sunken fire pit; dianthus and catmint fill in the bed. The combination of cottage-garden flowers with contemporary hardscape brings timeless warmth to a modern home.

left Severn's house was elevated from ground level because of the risk of flooding from a nearby river. That change in elevation provided for interesting landscaping opportunities. Here, French doors lead from the bedroom to a small patio and terraced rock garden planted with a mixture of edible and cutting plants. The rock was quarried from the nearby Salmon River.

Watching a plant first placed in the garden is a wonder. Is there something to be done to help it? Or should it just be watered and left alone for a time?

garden of plenty

These are questions that gardener Thomas Vetter asks each spring. And given that his 90-by-100-foot/27-by-30-meter suburban garden is filled to the brim with plants, he has plenty to wonder about.

For privacy, Vetter surrounded the perimeter with hedges and shrubs. Tall fir trees on the west side provide shade from the hot sun, and trelliess with vines screen out more of the nearby houses.

Dedicated gardener that he is, Vetter tries to plant, prune, weed, water, observe, or relax outside at least two hours at a time twice a day, all year long. During the winter he builds structures and assesses the bones of the garden. It's no wonder that there's always something blooming there.

Thomas Vetter says his favorite time of year is autumn, when his tropical favorites are at their peak, and other blossoms, berries, and foliage are deep with fall color. In mid-August, hints of fall's earth tones start to emerge in this screening group of plants including *Clematis* 'Golden Tiara', *Lonicera nitida* 'Baggesen's Gold', *Rudbeckia fulgida sullivantii* 'Goldsturm', *Catananche caerulea* (top), *Helianthus annuus* 'Lemon Queen', *Calamagrostis* 'Karl Foerster', and *Solidago rugosa* 'Fireworks' (bottom).

right There are many ways to make a suburban garden seem larger. Curved walking areas look as if they extend indefinitely. Along the way, interesting groups of plants, garden art, or an inviting chair encourage the stroller to linger.

below A cross-hatch of brick and stone leads through a perennial bed to a wooden arbor that Vetter made. Building is his 'winter hobby,' and he has crafted objects ranging from arbors to copper trellises and birdhouses. Come summer, he surrounded this creation with chartreuse and purple plants with variegated leaves.

above In a shadier spot, Vetter blended lilacs and rhododendrons, a 'Nikko Blue' hydrangea, *Fuchsia magellanica* 'Aurea', and *Verbascum olympicum*. The spiky flowering stem of the verbascum leads the eye to a dark beauty in the background, *Ensete ventricosum* 'Maurellii', or purple banana.

A GOOD URBAN GARDEN GETS YOU OUT OF TOWN FAST, AT LEAST IN THE META-
PHYSICAL SENSE. YOU CAN TURN EVEN A SMALL SPACE INTO A GETAWAY.

town

If you can see the universe in a flower, good—an urban garden
should transport you to realms beyond imagination, where the
garden's horizons are not limited by the walls of the house next door.

In urban settings, where space is tight, garden wherever you can:
in windows, up trellises, and on decks, balconies, and roofs. You'll
quickly learn that with a steady supply of water and fertilizer (slow-
release works best), large plants can grow in modest containers.
You can grow strawberries in a hanging basket, keeping the fruit
absolutely free of damage from slugs and sow bugs. Country
gardeners should be so lucky.

Indoor gardening also becomes essential. Houseplants purify the
air, and let you work with a range of tropical plants that would be
impossible to grow outdoors. You become intimate with moth
orchids and a bevy of bromeliads. It isn't bad, this urban gardening.
And it gets you away from the city.

A solitary cherub greets visitors to Robyn Cannon's hillside Seattle garden. The little fellow
is surrounded by a few other formal touches: brick, boxwood, and 'Sally Holmes' roses (left). The rich red
of mottled brick, mottled with moss, shows up the colors of the colorful potted flowers in Tamara Crocker and
Randy Sell's garden (top). Without the light-colored foliage of herbs and bright blossoms of dahlias, the dark
green ivy wall could cast this courtyard into gloom.

right A densely planted small garden can appear cluttered, unless corners and spaces are left for guests to stop, take a breath, and look for small surprises and unusual combinations. David Gemes created just such a spot in this corner, where visitors can delight in the blue oat grass, 'Pink Stripe' New Zealand flax, and a potted *Aeonium arboreum* 'Zwartkop'. Nestled above the white flowers of the Asiatic lily 'Little White Kiss' and the accompanying pink daylilies is a red banana plant.

below Formality and traditional elements work well in town gardens, especially those of older homes. Throughout her garden, Robyn Cannon has created perfect vignettes, such as this one, where 'Sally Holmes' roses and a Japanese maple also serve to screen the house next door.

left Tropical and Mediterranean influences in the Gemes garden include a neatly trimmed olive tree, scarlet yarrow, and another spiky flax (this one is 'Dusky Chief'); the containers themselves continue the theme. Climbing roses and a fence with a pattern of open squares give privacy without creating a solid barricade.

left A quiet corner in a hectic world—that's what even the smallest urban garden can provide. This contemplative spot contains a simple weatherworn teak chair and an intriguing wooden screen.

below This 1906 Victorian in Seattle's Queen Anne district was covered with white vinyl siding when Brian Coleman and Howard Cohen bought it; their extensive renovation included construction of a turret inscribed with a Latin quote translated as, "The more the better." Designers Glenn Withey and Charles Price took this advice to heart and created an extravaganza of a garden that includes ornate window boxes, overflowing containers, and colorful foliage and flowers to complement the owners' work. In this view, it's hard to imagine any more eye-popping texture and color until you realize that the passion vine over the porch is not yet in bloom.

small spaces

"How come you have every plant on earth in your little garden and it doesn't look like a mishmash?" That's a question people frequently ask Ciscoe Morris—the jovial master gardener, tour leader, radio-TV garden expert, and former head gardener (for 24 years) at Seattle University—who regales audiences with his horticultural adventures. "My goal is to have one of every plant on earth," he says in his impish Wisconsin accent, referring to the small city garden he shares with his wife, Mary. "We each have our own territories, 'cause we argue. But the two blend well."

Small as it may be, but it's big enough for vegetables, berries, flowers, and trees. "I love trees with a mad passion," says Morris. "When I first came to the Northwest, I'd go outdoors during windy weather and see these huge things blowing and think, 'I'm outta here.' Now I've fallen in love with them."

He also loves rocks ("they add stability to a garden"), and recalls the time he stuck a 2,000-pounder through the side of his house instead of in its intended spot. "It almost ruined my marriage," he says. "I go to Backhoe Anonymous now."

So how does he do so much in a small space? By squeezing in plants and growing dwarf forms. Fragrant trumpet lilies, which love having their roots in shade, grow up through ground covers, as do alliums. "I plant clematis on anything that stands still," he adds. "I once tried to plant one on my dog Koki, but she moved."

His favorite small tree? A Hinoki cypress he's grown for 20 years. ("I named it Fred, 'cause it looks like a guy I once knew. Kinda happy Buddha face and a big tummy.") And he tucks small plants between pavers.

He uses art and water features sparingly. Birdbaths are tucked away to protect little birds from passing hawks. His favorite water feature, "Bark Man," holds a basin in his mouth. There's even a place for Koki. "She likes to bury her rump in the soil, so we put down river stones wherever we don't want her to sit."

"One more thing," adds Morris. "Don't forget to surprise the living tweedle out of people. Make the backyard different than the front, so they'll stop in their tracks. Add an intimate spot where you can eat and enjoy a glass of wine. Live in your garden. It's where the hummingbirds are, and the mason bees buzz around, and the birds come to bathe. It's the coup de grâce."

What's next for the Morris garden? Stay tuned. "I'm constantly moving plants around." Besides, adds this joyful gardener, "I found Paradise when I came here. You can grow every plant on earth in the Northwest."

❧ CREATE GARDEN ROOMS. Break up the space with paths and hedges. "Decide how much you want to garden. If the lawn's too big, make it smaller. If it's not in the right spot, move it to a sunnier location."

❧ MAKE PATHS CURVY. A straight path from the curb to the front door says "Get in the house." But a curving path creates nooks and crannies for tucking in plants. And forget about a path that goes nowhere. Put a bench and an arbor at the end to make it a destination.

❧ CHOOSE THE RIGHT TREES. They should be in proportion. A tall house needs a tall tree beside it (an Italian cypress or 'Skyrocket' juniper, for instance).

❧ AGE YOUR STONES. "Moss makes a rock look like it's been there for a thousand years," says Morris. Choose rocks and boulders that aren't shiny, and have no moss on them (that moss usually dies when you get the rock home). In fall before rains come, make your own moss mixture. Pour one-third buttermilk and two-thirds water into a blender, then add moss from the garden ("when your partner's not home") and blend well. Pour or brush the mixture onto the rock.

INFLUENCED BY THE GARDENS OF ENGLAND AND ITALY, MARK HENRY HAS
TRANSFORMED A SMALL LOT INTO A SERIES OF GARDEN ROOMS.

SNOHOMISH, WA

urban influence

When Henry first saw his garden, it was an uninspired and ordinary lot just 120 by 100 feet/36 by 30 meters, filled with overgrown trees. Now, the structure and beauty in his garden is the result of wonderful soil and lots of pruning, hand-watering, pot moving, and an annual layering of compost. And, of course, a vision.

Henry's love for his garden is put to the test each winter when he moves the majority of his pots inside. Some plants are put in his cold frame, most are stored in a borrowed section of a friend's greenhouse, and flowering maples are placed on a table in the dining room window. Each year he swears he isn't going to pack and unpack so many plants, but each year he is tempted by new visions for the coming of spring.

Henry likes to collect different kinds of plants and mix formal plantings with informal ones. Some of his favorites, shown here, are hydrangeas and a *Rosa glauca*, on the right. The formal boxwood hedges and brick walk lead to a birdbath surrounded by potted topiaries of variegated boxwood. But further along, a bit of whimsy awaits— blue bottles slipped over the branches of a dead wisteria.

left and below Seating areas and potted plants are moved around as color ebbs and flows. This south side spot is one of only two sunny locations in the entire garden. Here Henry plants layers of hot tropicals like *Canna* 'Tropicanna', *C.* 'Pretoria', *Dahlia* 'Bishop of Landaff', and yellow angel's trumpet. A couple of Irish junipers, a hardy substitute for Italian cypress, add another touch of European presence to this garden room. And when umbrellas begin to show wear, he rejuvenates them with a layer of brightly colored latex paint.

below Irish juniper, boxwood, topiaries, and antique roses fit into a circular bed. The delicate Katsura tree in the background adds a touch of fun, lightening up the grouping. The tree's foliage changes color throughout the year, emerging reddish purple in spring, and turning bluish green in summer, then blushing apricot in fall.

above Henry lives on a busy street. A 10-ft/3-m hedge stops the hard city surfaces at the gate, marking the start of his garden. Straight ahead are the front porch and steps of Henry's bungalow—a perfect staging area for a *Helleborus argutifolius* and his collections of flowering maple, coleus, fuchsia, and hardy geraniums.

roof top

Just because you've moved to an apartment building or condominium doesn't mean you have to give up gardening. For one thing, you're likely to have a good view. Second, most rooftops and balconies provide a measure of privacy, far from barking dogs and passing traffic. With some creativity and a little planning, you can create your own sanctuary in the sky.

Indeed, in some parts of the world, green rooftops in urban areas are required by law for their environmental, economic, and social benefits. As Glen Patterson (whose spectacular rooftop garden appears on page 86) puts it, "Living trees and plants absorb carbon dioxide for photosynthesis, and they contribute precious oxygen to the atmosphere. Green roofs act as insulation, reducing heating and cooling costs. In summer, roof garden plants can absorb rainfall, reducing runoff. Many other advantages include the potential for growing fruits and vegetables, providing a habitat for birds, and, of course, the transformation of urban ugliness to natural beauty."

facing page Steve Lorton's 15-by-25-ft/4.5-by-7.6-m Seattle garden is living proof that you don't need a lot of space to create a comfortable area for outdoor dining and entertaining. All you need are large pots, good soil, available water, and diligent enthusiasm. Container plantings are key: Lorton has included some larger shrubs such as crape myrtle, hypericum, and heathers. He jazzed things up with colorful ceramic balls and bright zinnias, helichrysum, gerberas, and snapdragons. To pull the whole garden together, certain plants are repeated, such as ivy geranium and cheery yellow *Bidens ferulifolia*.

above and left Designer Joani Carter was thinking of year-round use when she created this rooftop living space. The terra-cotta–colored concrete slab floor was painted to resemble carpeting. The furniture is long-lasting indoor/outdoor wicker. Potted shrubs and fresh herbs provide multi-season greenery. Other than the pink geraniums and a *Leptospermum*, all the plants and furnishings can be left out in any weather.

sky high

When the time came for Glen Patterson to leave his longtime garden (see page 45), the flurry of building in Vancouver's Coal Harbour caught his eye—especially its proximity to downtown and Stanley Park, and the stunning views. He reasoned that if he could get into a building with an available roof deck he could transplant the heart of his previous garden. The only problem: Nobody had ever attempted to move a garden filled with mature trees, granite boulders, and a koi pond on this scale before. We asked him how he did it.

❧ GET THE RIGHT PEOPLE ON BOARD. Patterson was smart enough to enlist the help of the building's architect, James Cheng. "When he saw the possibilities," says Patterson, "he went bananas." Engineers were consulted to increase the roof's load-bearing capacity and ensure that all building codes were met.

❧ PLAN AHEAD. Likewise, Patterson consulted his longtime friend, garden designer Jim Nakano, about moving choice specimens, some of them a century old, from a "free-to-grow" garden to a roof garden with a requirement for compact and contained roots. Nakano had enough notice to begin root-pruning the plants two years in advance. In January, when the trees were dormant, their root balls were bound in plastic strapping to retain the soil during the move as well as to restrain root growth in the future. They are like outdoor bonsai plants, and all seem to be thriving in their new home.

❧ DRAINAGE MUST BE FLAWLESS. A root-repellent roof membrane, a drain mat, rigid insulation, 3 in/7 cm of clear crushed granular drainage material, and a geotextile filter fabric were installed, all of it underneath the pond's heavy rubber liner, which was also enclosed in layers of concrete. Filters help to keep the pond clear and a submersible pump recycles the pond water every 24 hours.

❧ LIGHTEN THE LOAD. A custom lightweight soil mix was devised consisting of black lava rock, graded sand, coconut fiber for organic content, and other soil amendments. Artificial boulders were created by pressure-blowing cement into steel mesh forms, then texturing the surfaces with realistic crevices.

The actual move called for a crane with a 110-ft/33-m boom to lift 30 tons of soil mix, 25 tons of trees and plants, rocks, and other building materials. And although the initial costs and effort were high, Patterson is pleased. "The garden is a sustainable one with virtually no maintenance work," he says. "There are no lawns to mow, no hedges to clip; there is no room for weeds to grow; there are no slugs or deer; and the sprinklers are automatic."

facing page Patterson was able to transplant treasured specimens such as an 80-year-old Japanese black pine *(Pinus thunbergii)*. He says that visitors actually appreciate the tree's form more silhouetted against the surrounding skyscrapers than they did in his previous garden.

above Mushroom-colored, reproduction, Yorkshire paving stones provide a neutral surface for displaying plants and furniture in a garden overlooking Vancouver's English Bay. Plants are placed for emphasis and drama, including a stiff-leafed windmill palm *(Trachycarpus fortunei)*, New Zealand flax, cannas, and—draping out over a classical urn—*Molinia caerulea* 'Variegata'. {THOMAS HOBBS DESIGN}

A GARDEN INSPIRED BY THE GROTTOS OF ANCIENT ITALY, ACCOMPLISHED
THROUGH MODERN ENGINEERING, BECOMES A VILLA IN THE SKY.

VANCOUVER, B.C.

higher ground

Constant exposure to wind, lack of privacy, and a rotten roof membrane weren't going to stop Sid Dickens from building the garden of his imagination high over the city. For the first two problems he turned to traditional gardening solutions: a row of trees and a vine-covered arbor. The latter problem, however, meant he had to call in the help of the architectural landscape firm Artifolia. After raising the roof deck off the roof, the builders supported it with steel beams and then surrounded it with planters. Although they're actually 4 feet/ 1.2 meters high, the raised roof deck makes the planters seem like they're at roof level—an illusion that enhances the feeling of being in a "real" garden.

Then began the fun work—filling the garden with plants, furniture, a water feature, and the gardener's love of fanciful artistry.

The plants on many roof gardens suffer from too much exposure to sun and wind. By building a large pergola and covering it with fast-growing Algerian ivy, and installing an automatic watering system, Dickens has created moist, shady conditions to encourage plenty of mossy growth.

left All gardens employ the art of illusion to some extent, but Dickens has done a truly masterful job. Although this tiled floor resembles a Roman mosaic, in fact, artist Wade King sponge-painted the tiles onto wood, then sealed the entire piece with an exterior sealer. Real tile would have been too heavy for the roof to bear.

above Dickens has always had a close connection to the sea and surrounds himself with objects that remind him of childhood fishing trips. This face of Bacchus wears a shell-and-coral crown. He is made of real concrete, but elsewhere the planters are constructed of wood and coated with a thin layer of plaster; again, the objective is to keep down the weight on the roof.

left A similarly decorated pot (made by Dickens' mother) holds a small heather. The watery theme is continued throughout the garden; the fountain is also barnacled with shells.

mediterranean

In these southern European gardens, sturdy, heat-loving plants like lavender and rosemary grow around generously sized courtyards, patios, and terraces of concrete, flagstone, brick, gravel, or decomposed granite. Lawns are minimal or non-existent. Vine-covered arbors provide shade, and trickling fountains refresh the spirit as well as the senses.

Artful accessories add color and style. Glazed tiles line fountains or dress up walls. Pots are filled with flowers or displayed empty—a classic olive jar at the end of an allée or a stone urn atop a pedestal, for instance.

Mediterranean gardens are not just for southern Europeans. In Seattle and Vancouver, we've seen gardens whose designs were inspired by those in Sardinia or Provence, and filled with plants from similar climates, including South Africa, Australia, and Chile. Such gardens make sense for areas where the population is growing but water supplies are not.

Alliums with puffball flowerheads and blooming woolly lamb's ears blend together the soft grays and lavenders of a Mediterranean plant palette.

facing page Marnie MacNeill's house sits on a bluff overlooking Victoria's Oak Bay. Faced with recurring watering restrictions, MacNeill decided to turn her front yard into a gravel garden. She built raised beds and filled them with 12 in/30 m of soil, topped with a weed-suppressing fabric and 6 in/15 cm of gravel. After just one year, the drought-tolerant plants—such as cardoon, yarrows, lavenders, artemisia, and coreopsis—are thriving with no summer water.

below In the garden of Peter Symcox and Fernand Choquette in Metchosin, smoke tree and barberry spice a mostly green planting with autumnal hues; a potted yucca grows at left. In areas shaded by native pines and arbutus, peonies, heathers, and azaleas provide the color. Throughout the garden are potted geraniums, palms, and other tender specimens.

left A small-leafed shrub weaves through the burgundy leaves of *Canna* 'Australia' beside a railing overlooking an azure sea. Surprisingly, it's not the French Riviera; it's Vancouver's English Bay.
{DICKENS GARDEN}

THIS GARDEN PROVIDES ITS OWNER WITH THE MEDITERRANEAN AMBIENCE
AND AL FRESCO LIVING SHE LOVES.

coast med

It took Janet Dindia seven years to build the "bones" of her Mercer Island garden. Now she seizes every opportunity to be outside, enjoying the way the plants are filling in around that basic structure.

Dindia grew up in an Italian family that cultivated a wide variety of herbs, vegetables, and fruits—a tradition she continues with her large assortment of garden edibles. She loves to grill vegetables with fresh herbs, stuff zucchini blossoms, or prepare a simple plate of just-picked tomatoes and basil.

Edibles aren't the only plants in the garden, however. Dindia has experimented with various drought-tolerant plants from the Mediterranean, California, and elsewhere to see what will thrive in her coastal micro-climate. Those that have thrived include loquat, strawberry tree (*Arbutus unedo*), weeping pear, ceanothus, euphorbia, rockrose, and the box honeysuckle *Lonicera nitida* 'Baggesen's Gold.'

Looking down the steps into the courtyard with its backdrop of Douglas fir reminds Dindia of the Tuscan hills; perhaps that's why this is her favorite part of the garden. Flanking the top of the steps are spires of potted *Juniperus communis* 'Compressa'. Tumbling down the slope are heat-lovers like ceanothus, Russian sage, rockrose, and *Senecio greyi*. Beside the water feature, a thriving fig tree shelters a half-hidden chaise longue.

right Meals are served outside whenever possible. The simple wooden arbor supports a canopy of cool-season grapes ('Glenora', 'Interlaken', and 'Canadice') rather than 'Zinfandel', but the effect is much the same. Fragrant rosemary and honeysuckle surround the terrace. In a terraced garden below is a vegetable garden filled with artichokes, leeks, berries, and salad greens.

below The slender curves of this antique French bench are echoed by spires of lemon verbena and Russian sage (Perovskia). Behind the bench is a locust tree (Robinia pseudoacacia 'Frisia'); an Elaeagnus pungens 'Fruitlandii' has been clipped into a neat ball, which contrasts nicely with the more wispy plants in the scene.

above The upper patio contains another dining spot, this one overlooking Lake Washington. The foreground mix of plants includes sea holly (Eryngium), agapanthus, and daisy-flowered Rudbeckia nitida.

The FLAMBOYANCE OF A TROPICAL GARDEN ISN'T FOR EVERYONE. BUT IT'S PERFECT FOR THOSE GARDENERS WHO YEARN FOR THE AMBIENCE OF A WARM, MOIST JUNGLE, BRIGHT COLORS, AND A LITTLE DRAMA.

tropical

Big leaves, dense planting, and bright colors—not frost tenderness—define tropical gardens. That's why we are so fond of cannas and giant petasites. Skillfully blended with bamboo, ferns, Chinese windmill palms, and a big-leafed rhododendron, these outsized (even outrageous) plants can make the garden feel more like San Diego than San Juan Island.

But there are two important caveats for gardeners who want to cultivate a tropical retreat in this corner of North America. First, because wind shreds big leaves, you'll succeed only if your garden is relatively protected. Second, big-leafed plants are generally thirsty, so don't try this planting style if water is in short supply in your community.

That said, start experimenting with big-leafed and brightly colored plants that are perfectly hardy, as well as ones that aren't. If you have a greenhouse or sunroom, include exotics such as angel's trumpet *(Brugmansia),* bird of Paradise, or bougainvillea.

Don't be afraid to bring a little sizzle to the garden with painted walls and brightly colored containers, water features, and ornaments. That's what Des Kennedy did in this corner "hot spot," where silver-leafed snow-in-summer makes its way to a *Euphorbia mellifera.*

above When soft, filtered light hits this tropical planting in front of Linda Cochran's Bainbridge Island house, the Mexican feather grass seems to come alive in softly floating waves that complement the larger leaves of palms and the brilliant bracts of potted bougainvillea.

left Tropical borders look lushest when tightly packed with dramatic combinations of plants. Ben Hammontree built this composition in layers: Japanese banana (Musa basjoo), blackwood acacia (Acacia melanoxylon), and empress tree (Paulownia tomentosa), at the back; Amaranthus cruentus, with its drooping tassels, in front; and staggered drifts of Canna 'Red King Humbert' along the length of the border.

STRUCTURE, DECOR, AND PLANTS COMBINE TO HEAT UP A FORMERLY
BLAND NORTHWEST GARDEN.

VANCOUVER, B.C.

hot enough

When Thomas Hobbs and Brent Beattie moved to their 1930s Spanish Revival home in Vancouver, they wanted to heat up the property with the vibrant tones and colorful plants of the tropics. One of the first

tasks was to pick a color scheme for the stuccoed house walls: Hobbs chose a warm terra-cotta. Over time, they replaced the existing rhododendrons and perennial borders with a vivid mixture of colorful plants with jagged, knobby, or striking textures that complement the house architecture. Tender plants are kept in containers, brought inside during winter, and placed beside sunny windows. The effect is one of intoxicating abundance. Says Hobbs, "I have a no-bare-earth policy."

A garden like this does not spring up overnight. You can achieve a similar effect over time by starting with one spot in your garden. Choose a theme, and begin placing and rearranging plants to please your eye. Paint a wall, fill pots to overflowing with exotic succulents, and don't be afraid to experiment.

One of Hobbs's favorite plant families is the echeverias. Scattered throughout the garden are his "pizzas"—shallow containers filled with E. × imbricata, aeoniums, and other succulents. But such containers are not just plunked down anywhere. Groupings of odd-numbered pots of various heights but similar tones and styles are carefully placed throughout the garden. In this grouping, a potted New Zealand flax is placed so the sun can illuminate its deep maroon-scarlet spears.

clockwise from top These steps, that lead nowhere, were once part of a clothesline area. Beattie used slate and tiles in blues, grays, and rusts to create a lovely staging area for these potted jewels. A curved terra-cotta–colored wall shelters a protected grouping of hostas, *Cimicifuga simplex* 'Brunette', and a dark *Helleborus orientalis*; in the foreground are more succulent "pizzas." This fiery grouping includes the scarlet Asiatic lily 'Cosmic Blast', a variegated dwarf canna ('Pink Sunburst'), a burgundy-blushed *Lilium* 'Lovelite', and *Anthemis tinctoria* 'Sauce Hollandaise'.

IT'S NO IDLE BOAST TO SAY THAT EVERY NORTHWEST GARDEN IS EITHER SUNNY ENOUGH FOR HERBS, HAS ENOUGH WINTER CHILL FOR STONE FRUITS, OR IS MILD ENOUGH TO GROW VEGETABLES YEAR-ROUND.

edible

With few exceptions (such as winter pears and kiwis), the world's tastiest fruits and vegetables are those from your own garden. Sweet corn and fresh peas, for example, are sugar-sweet the moment you harvest them, but start getting starchy from that point on; alpine strawberries—those fraises du bois so beloved by the French—have a shelf life of only a few hours; and vine-ripened tomatoes are perfectly scrumptious…until you put them in the fridge.

Well-planned food gardens bear crops continually from spring's first asparagus spears until frost puts the sweetness in autumn kale. West of the Cascades, you can even harvest leaf and root vegetables through winter.

Northwest food gardens can be conventional straight rows in flat gardens, but more often they're raised up into beds of enriched earth, artfully displayed in containers, or skillfully blended into the perennial border.

Northwest gardeners find ingenious ways to tuck in a few heads of lettuce or some herbs for the kitchen. The angled beds in this house overlooking Lake Washington hold just enough greens and squash to provide the owners with fresh garden produce daily.

above The fruits and vegetables in Phoebe Noble's 2-acre Saanich garden are tended by her daughter, Sandra Holloway, who uses many of the same principles employed by her mother elsewhere in the garden. First among them is to use plenty of mulch — compost, wood chips, or straw (shown here) — to help keep moisture in and weeds down. The bamboo used for this bean trellis is grown on the property.

above right In the Holloway garden, scarlet runner beans clamber up a traditional tepee. Beans and peas are among the easiest and most prolific plants to grow in the Northwest.

right This small pathway leads through a mixed planting in the garden of Karin Ristou and Chris Weixelbaumer. Behind the rhubarb plant, salad greens such as mesclun grow amid flowers and herbs.

AN ISLAND FARM GROWS A LITTLE BIT OF EVERYTHING, MAKING FOR PLENTY
OF FRESH FOOD AND PRODUCE OF ALL KINDS.

LOPEZ ISLAND, WA

garden farm

Some islands are known for their abundant fresh produce and other farm products; Lopez Island is one of them. Red Gate Farm is certainly prolific. Read and Marianne Langenbach raise Suffolk sheep, breed llamas, grow fruit trees (apple, cherry, pear, and fig), and have constructed a well-defended vegetable plot that is a garden in itself.

The fence around the kitchen garden is a barrier, with two layers of field fencing above and chicken wire below. The grazing animals make their contribution to the garden, however, as composted manure is applied liberally to amend the soil.

This is the view from the Langenbachs' house; past the kitchen garden and the pasture toward Puget Sound. Approximately half of the property is woodland and half is pasture, with one acre of orchards and about one-fifth of an acre devoted to the kitchen garden.

left The vegetable bed brims with red cabbage, broccoli, squash, and potatoes. The Langenbachs have experimented to see which plants are best started from seed and which need a head start in six-packs. Tomatoes need to get started in the greenhouse and so are always planted out of nursery containers.

below An old stock-watering trough was recycled into a central focal point, filled with reeds and horsetails, and run with a solar-powered pump. The pathways in the garden are made of crushed oyster shells collected on the beaches of a nearby island. They remind Marianne of her childhood visits to Cape Cod; they also reflect heat that is much appreciated by the lavender at the base of the trough.

above An 'Interlaken' grape grows out of an appropriate wine barrel, trained up crisscrossed wire mesh fencing. Around the base of the container grow 'Six Hills Giant' catmint (Nepeta), annual cosmos, and crown-pinks.

right Mixing edibles and ornamentals is not only attractive, but good for the garden, as the blend attracts an assortment of beneficial insects and pollinators. Here, Cosmos bipinnatus 'Sensation', 'Hidcote' lavender, scarlet runner beans, and artichokes mix with old-fashioned snapdragons.

complement rather than dominate the scene. An existing stand of large conifers make a dramatic border to the garden as the trees' dark hues illuminate the leaf colors of lighter-foliaged trees and shrubs. To lighten the texture of a grouping, plant fine-needled species such as hemlock or dawn redwood. To vary the color palette, add light blue Atlas cedar, silvery white pine, or blue-green giant redwood.

You can create striking combinations by contrasting conifers with broad-leafed shrubs and trees. Try vine and Japanese maples with western hemlock, or rhododendrons against a coniferous backdrop.

A few conifers such as dawn redwood and Alaska cedar will perform well in light shade. Western red cedar, dawn redwood, and bald cypress are among those that prefer moist sites. As a group, conifers rarely require pruning, but you may wish to thin or shape them to emphasize interesting branch patterns or to create space for other plants or views.

above Sometimes it's best to allow nature center stage. Tall native conifers form a curtain backdrop to this serene garden on Whidbey Island, essentially a grassy clearing in the woods. {DEBORAH HEG GARDEN}

conifers

LARGE (70+ FT/21+ M)

Incense cedar *Calocedrus decurrens*
Blue Atlas cedar *Cedrus atlantica* 'Glauca'
Dawn redwood *Metasequoia glyptostroboides*
Japanese black pine *Pinus thunbergii*
Coast redwood *Sequoia sempervirens*
Giant sequoia *Sequoiadendron giganteum*
Bald cypress *Taxodium distichum*

SMALL TO MEDIUM (40–60 FT/12–18 M)

Korean fir *Abies koreana*
Alaska cedar *Chamaecyparis nootkatensis,*
    C. n. 'Pendula'
Slender hinoki cypress *C. obtusa* 'Gracilis'
Serbian spruce *Picea omorika*
Umbrella pine *Sciadopitys verticillata*
American arborvitae *Thuja occidentalis* 'Fastigiata'
False arborvitae *Thujopsis dolabrata*
Mountain hemlock *Tsuga mertensiana*

DECIDUOUS TREES DO MUCH MORE THAN BLOCK THE SUN. THEY GIVE US
BRILLIANT COLORS IN FALL BEFORE THE LEAVES DISAPPEAR FOR THE WINTER.

deciduous trees

When planted next to the south and west sides of a house, deciduous trees moderate summer heat but allow in winter sunlight. And with their statuesque nature, many of these trees lend a feeling of age and permanence to a garden.

What is the biggest consideration when choosing a tree? Its eventual height. The largest trees might shade the entire side of a house, while those 40 feet/12 meters or less serve as cool natural umbrellas over a patio or entryway.

Although maples (page 110–111) and oaks represent the largest number of Northwest deciduous trees, other species also have qualities to offer. Some suggestions are listed here.

above The massive trunks of native bigleaf maple (*Acer macrophyllum*) make it too large for a small garden or street tree, but it's magnificent in a naturalistic garden setting. Its huge leaves—often up to a foot wide—turn a brilliant yellow in fall.

right Victoria's Oak Bay neighborhood is named for the Garry oaks that lend its streets such charm. This ancient specimen towers over a corner of Terry LeBlanc's garden. Underneath, she has planted a collection of shade-loving rhododendrons and hostas.

Dove tree

trees

LARGE (70+ FT/21+ M)

European beech *Fagus sylvatica*
　　　'Laciniata'
Copper beech *F.s.* 'Atropunicea'
Ginkgo *Ginkgo biloba*
　　　'Autumn Gold'
Tulip tree *Liriodendron tulipifera*
Scarlet oak *Quercus coccinea*
Garry oak *Q. garryana*
Red oak *Q. rubra*

SMALLER (UNDER 60 FT/18 M)

Red maple *Acer rubrum* 'October
　　　Glory', 'Red Sunset',
　　　'Sun Valley'
European hornbeam
　　　Carpinus betulus
Dove tree *Davidia involucrata*
Yulan magnolia *Magnolia denudata*
Sour gum *Nyssa sylvatica*
Willow oak *Quercus phellos*
Korean mountain ash
　　　Sorbus alnifolia
Whitebeam *S. aria*
Sawleaf zelkova *Zelkova serrata*

pruning trees
Cass Turnbull doesn't mince words. "I hate bad pruning," says the outspoken Seattle gardener who founded PlantAmnesty in 1987 to promote proper shrub and tree care. Turnbull has seen many beauties reduced to beasts by thoughtless whacking: a giant sequoia with just a few branches and needles left along its trunk; conifers sheared; oak trees topped; shrubs buzz-sawed into balls and cubes (exception: clipped hedges and topiaries in formal gardens). "I would be embarrassed to make a mistake like that in front of the whole world," she says. "It's like paying someone to dent your car."

But of all the injustices done to trees, perhaps the worst are committed to expose views. "I've seen 60-foot poplars cut in half," she says. "Clearcutting around streams, so they dried up and blackberries took over. Trees that were girdled or poisoned."

"This obsession with water views has undermined our good work," laments Turnbull. Mature trees are, after all, your landscape's most valuable assets. They improve air quality and keep bluffs from sliding into the sound. Placed to block hot summer sun, they can provide natural air conditioning. They frame views, and make beautiful silhouettes against the night sky.

"The goal of any pruning," says Turnbull, "should be to maintain the long term health, beauty, and safety of the tree." Pay special attention to trees that water-sprout easily, such as cherry, dogwood, Japanese laceleaf maple, magnolia, and witch hazel, as heavy pruning subverts their elegant branch structures.

So if the trees on your property block your view, try one of the strategies below. At all costs, don't top the tree; you'll spoil it forever. If you can't do the work yourself, call an arborist certified by the International Society of Arborists (ISA). For additional information, contact PlantAmnesty, Box 15377, Seattle 98115-0377 or www.plantamnesty.org.

❧ WINDOWING. Open up the tree by removing just a few lateral branches, creating windows through which to see the distance.

❧ THINNING. Selectively thin a midrange tree to open up views and reduce its "sail area." First clear out bunches of foliage and smaller branches, also branches that are weak, dead, or crossing. When you can see the overall branch structure, prune along the main limbs. Leave a natural-looking, bushy top.

❧ SKIRTING UP. To reveal a view without ruining the lines of a tree, remove some lower limbs. Don't skirt up more than one-third of the tree.

❧ REMOVAL. If pruning won't open up views, consider having the offending trees removed. But keep some trees on the edges of your outlook to frame the view.

TWO NORTHWEST NATIVES, THE BIGLEAF MAPLE AND THE VINE MAPLE, REPRESENT
THE MIGHTIEST AND ALSO THE MOST DELICATE OF THE GENUS *ACER.*

maples

When it comes to maples, Northwesterners don't stop with the homegrown.
After all, maples in all their forms and glories sweep across the globe's
northern latitudes. (Little wonder Canadians have honored the maple leaf
on their flag.) Northwest streets are lined with stately maples from Norway
and the American Northeast. Species from China etch strong lines against
our gray winter skies. Japanese maples soften the harsh edges of buildings.
Century-old specimens stretch over massive boulders in the front lawns of
Portland and Seattle. Others overhang ponds where colorful fish glide in
their dappled shade.

Maples reward us with four seasons of beauty. From sculptural winter
forms, plump red buds emerge in early spring to open into a lacy canopy.
Next come the diminutive, but beautiful, flowers, some of which turn into
winged seeds, fluttering along with the slightest breeze, landing on lawns

above A red laceleaf Japanese maple sets the canopy and the earth beneath on fire when it turns color in fall.
Deeply cut leaves of green, orange, or purplish red, and a weeping form characterize laceleaf maples.
left For smaller spaces, dwarf trees such as 'Red Pygmy' take well to container culture, or even for bonsai specimens.

and patios like tiny birds. Summer brings heavier shade and the comforting rustle of leaves. And fall ignites the glowing hues for which maples are most famous.

Relatively free of pests and happy in a variety of growing conditions, maples require little more than light pruning and raking of the seed in early summer and leaves in fall. If you've never grown a maple, pick a spot in your garden, choose a plant that fits the space, and put it in the ground. If you already have a maple or two in your garden, plant another one.

great maples

Vine maple *Acer circinatum:* Best grown in clumps where its asymmetrical trunks can stretch up to 5 to 35 ft/ 3 to 11 m.

David's maple *Acer davidii:* A garden-scale maple (reaching 30 to 35 ft/9 to 11 m), with handsome bark which is shiny, green striped with silvery white.

Paperbark maple *Acer griseum:* A striking specimen in winter, when its reddish bark curls and peels.

Japanese maple *Acer palmatum:* From coral barked 'Sango Kaku' to the dramatic burgundy leaves of 'Bloodgood', all are known for their delicate scale and autumn color.

Norway maple *Acer platanoides:* Plant on the south or west side of the house, where it will stretch up to 50 ft/15 m and spread to shade the house in summer, then defoliate to let winter sun stream through its branches.

Scarlet maple *Acer rubrum:* Tall and wide, this plant makes an excellent street tree and is famous for its fall color.

Sugar maple *Acer saccharinum:* Several named varieties make this 60-ft/18-m maple a much-loved shade tree with the bonus of spectacular autumn color.

Amur maple *Acer tataricum ginnala:* Not widely known, this unsung star has a manageable scale (15 to 20 ft/ 4.5 to 6 m high and wide) and a brilliant fall show of red foliage.

above Distinctive for its multiple trunks, vine maple sports soft green foliage in spring and summer, and among the Northwest's loveliest colors in fall.
below The cinnamon-colored peeling bark of paperbark maple glows when backlit. Plant it where low morning or afternoon light can shine through.

above An unusually modest Japanese maple (*Acer palmatum* 'Ukigumo') has leaves of cream and green tinged with pink, giving it a romantic appeal.

TREES AND UNDERSTORY SHRUBS ARE THE BACKBONE OF A LOW-MAINTENANCE GARDEN, WHERE MORE DEMANDING PERENNIALS AND ANNUALS CAN BE TUCKED INTO SPACES BETWEEN THEM.

understory

Woody plants that grow in the 15-to-30-foot/4-to-9-meter range make ideal candidates for smaller, more shaded backyards. As a group, these understory plants can be matched to every soil and weather condition the Northwest offers, wet to dry, sun to shade. Because of their smaller stature, they are ideal for blocking unwanted views without overwhelming the rest of the garden. And, with a wide variety of flowers, leaf shapes, and sizes, these plants bring form and texture into the garden.

Some, like hydrangeas, have spectacular flowers. Others are valued for their colorful foliage or fruit. The gray-green leaves and bright red berries of cotoneasters stand out in front of dark fir trees, and the brilliant maroon barberry (*Berberis thunbergii* 'Rose Glow') makes a strong accent wherever it is placed. Variegated black elder (*Sambucus nigra* 'Madonna') brightens the landscape on the dullest days. For fall color, small specimen trees like the elegant weeping katsura (*Cercidiphyllum japonicum* 'Pendulum') shim-

mer. And in the winter garden, the bare stems of the blood-twig dogwood (*Cornus sanguinea* 'Midwinter Fire') blaze yellow, orange, and red.

Many of these undemanding plants are also fragrant. In milder areas, groundcover sweet box *(Sarcococca hookerana humilis)* opens tiny blossoms that scent the whole garden in January. In colder regions, gardeners enjoy the fragrance of hardy mock orange hybrids like *Philadelphus* × *virginalis* 'Minnesota Snowflake'.

woodland fragrance

Wintersweet *Chimonanthus praecox*
Fringe tree *Chionanthus virginicus*
Mexican orange *Choisya ternata*
Harlequin glorybower
    Clerodendrum trichotomum
Summersweet *Clethra alnifolia* 'Pink Spires'
Sweet fern *Comptonia peregrina*
Fragrant winter hazel *Corylopsis glabrescens*
Daphne × *burkwoodii*
Garland daphne *D. cneorum*
Winter daphne *D. odora*
Deutzia corymbosa
Paper bush *Edgeworthia chrysantha*
Eucryphia lucida 'Pink Cloud'
Sweetspire *Itea virginica* 'Henry's Garnet'
Sargent crabapple *Malus sargentii*
Banana shrub *Michelia figo*
Delavay osmanthus *Osmanthus delavayi*
Sweet olive *O. fragrans aurantiacus*
Sweet mock orange *Philadelphus coronarius*
P. × *purpureomaculatus* 'Belle Etoile'
P. × *virginalis* 'Minnesota Snowflake'
Flowering plum *Prunus* × *blireiana*
Rhododendron edgeworthii 'Bodnant'
Sweet box *Sarcococca hookerana humilis*
S. ruscifolia
Texas mountain laurel *Sophora secundiflora*
Fragrant snowbell *Styrax obassia*
Cutleaf lilac *Syringa* × *laciniata*
Sweet viburnum *Viburnum awabukii*
V. × *bodnantense* 'Pink Dawn'
Korean spice viburnum *V. carlesii*

facing page, top Weeping katsura (*Cercidiphyllum japonicum* 'Pendulum') is draped in a bright gold curtain that lasts for several weeks in this Eugene garden. facing page, bottom A series of layered shrubs, small trees, and grasses step down under tall conifers and a laburnum- and wisteria-covered arbor. above, top *Viburnum plicatum tomentosum* is among the most beautiful of the viburnums, with horizontal tiers of white blossoms in spring. above Puffs of fragrant white flowers in spring and yellow to scarlet fall color appear on *Fothergilla major.* right Fall and winter color in the understory can take the form of bright red berries, as on this *Cotoneaster lacteus.*

IT'S HARD TO IMAGINE THE NORTHWEST WITHOUT RHODODENDRONS AND AZALEAS. UNPARALLELED AMONG FLOWERING SHRUBS IN THEIR DIVERSITY, IT'S LITTLE WONDER THEY ARE SUCH A MAINSTAY.

rhododendrons

The commonly held image of masses of large round evergreen shrubs loaded with big, colorful trusses in spring is only a tiny aspect of rhododendron's potential. The Pacific rhododendron *(Rhododendron macrophyllum),* Washington's state flower, occurs from northern California to southern British Columbia. Western azalea *(R. occidentale),* of which there are many hybrids but which is a beautiful shrub in its own right, mixes gracefully with rhododendrons and other evergreens. And garden centers stock a large selection of both Asiatic species and locally hybridized varieties.

The flowering season for rhododendrons stretches from February, when *R. mucronulatum* blooms, to August, which brings forth the fragrant white trusses of *R. auriculatum.* Because rhododendrons look best when contrasted with the textures and colors of other plants, plant them alongside bulbs and flowering trees with comparable bloom periods. Most rhododendrons bloom for just a short time, so choose forms with beautiful plant structure and leaf color or texture. Play large leaves against small ones, round against narrow. In fall, enrich the colors of adjacent trees with deciduous types whose

above Blue spring bloom and bronze new foliage is typical of *Rhododendron augustinii* hybrids, such as 'Crater Lake'.
right Deciduous azaleas massed in a shrubs border harmonize beautifully when their colors are on the muted side, and carefully distributed.

autumn leaves blaze in shades of red, orange, and yellow.

Broad pathways and winding grass corridors are especially inviting when they're lined with tall rhododendrons (to 6 feet/2 meters), backed by taller trees. Use lower-growing rhododendrons (to 3 feet/1 meter) along entry gardens, and dwarf forms (under 1 foot/30 centimeters) as groundcover or rock garden specimens. Deciduous azaleas in a mixed shrub border provide a spotlight of bloom and fall color, blending into the background the rest of the season.

Larger-leafed evergreen rhododendrons lend themselves well to the light shade of woodland settings. Azaleas and the deciduous and small-leafed evergreen rhododendrons (whose foliage is often fragrant) will take more sunlight. Rich, slightly acidic, well-drained soils with healthy layers of mulch and some summer water are essential for most of them. Some of the deciduous azaleas prefer damper soils, and the Mediterranean evergreen azalea cultivars are quite drought tolerant.

Unfortunately, some pests and diseases such as black vine weevil, *Phytophthora* root rot, and rhododendron powdery mildew, can thrive here as strongly as the genus itself. Their influence can be diminished through attention to proper placement and culture, and by selecting those less prone to these plagues.

above Individual blossoms of *Rhododendron calendulaceum*. right Many deciduous azaleas offer a splendid fall color display. *R. luteum* is one of the showiest.

greer When 9-year-old Harold Greer showed up at meetings of the Men's Camellia and Rhododendron Society in Eugene, its members must have suspected they had a child prodigy in their midst. The last 50 years have proven them right, as anybody who has grown a 'Trude Webster' or 'Hallelujah' rhododendron could tell you; both are among the best in their color classes.

Greer introduced these and many other rhododendrons, and helped fuel the interest in rhododendrons and their companion plants. Outside the Himalayas, there are few better places in the world to grow rhododendrons than in the mild Northwest, where woodland shade, abundant rainfall, and moderate temperatures make perfect habitat. Greer should know: his plant-related travels have taken him to Japan, Australia, New Zealand, and Europe.

How does this breeder see the future? "I like the yakushimanums very much. They're good looking and compact, so they fit well into smaller gardens. And breeders have done a lot of work to extend their flower colors—there are almost too many now.

"I also like the new bicolored rhododendron introductions: ones like 'Ring of Fire' from the Thompsons in Waldport, and 'Midnight Mystique' from Frank Fukuoka. There is also constant work to extend the hardiness range of rhododendrons, especially in yellow-flowered varieties."

Greer Gardens, 1280 Goodpasture Island Road, Eugene, OR 97401; or www.greergardens.com

DEGREES OF SHADE VARY FROM NEAR DARKNESS BELOW CEDARS AND BIGLEAF
MAPLES TO DAPPLED LIGHT BELOW BIRCH AND ASH TREES.

shade

Many Northwest gardens are sheltered by native trees, bringing welcome relief in summer but presenting a challenge to gardeners longing for light and color in the garden. Fortunately, many shade-loving perennials have flower or foliage color that can light up the darkness. Most of these plants flourish best where shade is cast by walls and fences, free from interfering tree roots, so that soil remains moist and fertile. Elsewhere, thin branches to admit light and rainfall, amend soil with compost, and mulch the ground to make dense shade more hospitable. In dry shade, choose vigorous perennials with deep roots and thick leaves, such as Mrs. Robb's bonnet *(Euphorbia amygdaloides robbiae)* or showy epimediums.

Hostas are unrivaled for bold foliage brushed with color. Those with white or golden edges or centers tend to bring a sense of warmth to the border; those with blue tones seem to tone it down. Pastel flowers and

silver-tinted leaves, or those that are variegated, gold, or blue-green light up the understory.

Brighten the front of the border with the colorful leaves of cyclamens, or of such coral bells (*Heuchera*) as wine-tinted 'Plum Pudding', icy green 'Mint Frost', or golden 'Amber Waves'. Provide contrast in shady borders by adding lacy ferns and by filling the mid-border with feathery plumes of *Astilbe* or masterwort (*Astrantia major*).

facing page The elegantly dissected leaves of *Sambucus racemosa* 'Sutherland Gold' illuminate this woodland scene along with the electric pink flowers of the showy lacecap 'Geoffrey Chadbund' hydrangea. above Elaine Whitehead scoured specialty nurseries for plants to put underneath her shade structure. Backed by a variegated ivy (*Hedera helix* 'Gold Heart'), the resulting lush collection includes *Sambucus racemosa* 'Plumosa Aurea', *Dryopteris* × *complexa* 'Robust', *Filipendula ulmaria* 'Aurea', *Hostas* 'Regal Splendour' and *H. sieboldiana* 'Elegans', and *Astrantia major* 'Sunningdale Variegated'. right Tom Vetter's shady retreat benefits from luminous foliage and contrasting textures, including golden-variegated *Aucuba japonica* 'Picturata', big blue-green *Hosta sieboldiana* 'Elegans', and lacy Korean rock fern.

below Even though bishop's hat (*Epimedium grandiflorum*) is deciduous, the purple tints in its new growth and the white flowers that hover gracefully above the leaves make it an invaluable shade groundcover.

above A protected spot is the place to show off 'Gold Heart' bleeding heart. Its shapely, luminous leaves and profusion of pink hearts command attention starting in spring and enduring through the summer months.

right Combinations of dark and light foliage really draw the eye. The vibrant pinkish-red flowers of 'Hadspen Blood' masterwort bring out the best in 'Brunette' bugbane's chocolate leaves.

above Dreamy as a watercolor, blue *Corydalis flexuosa* blends beautifully with white 'Vestal' wood anemone and grape hyacinths. These cool tones create a tranquil mood in the shade garden. right Softly upright, the wand-like leaves of 'Knight's Shades' golden sedge brighten this border's edge and offer a backdrop for delicate 'Blue Moonlight' violas.

left Copper and rose tints accentuate the fronds of autumn fern. *Houttuynia cordata* 'Chameleon' repeats the pink hue but offers an arresting contrast in leaf shape.

FROM PORT HARDY, B.C., TO EUREKA, CALIFORNIA, THESE APPEALING DWARF
SHRUBS ASK FOR NOTHING MORE THAN A SUNNY SITE, WELL-DRAINED BUT MOISTURE-
RETENTIVE SOIL, AND AN OCCASIONAL HAIRCUT.

heaths and heathers

Heaths and heathers deserve their difficult reputation only in extremely dry conditions or cold-winter/hot-summer regions, such as those east of the Cascades. Elsewhere, moist air, acidic soil, rainy winters, and temperate summers match their growing needs perfectly. In return, their flowers and foliage give us an ever-changing medley of soft colors, punctuated now and then by dazzlingly bright accents.

True Scotch heathers *(Calluna vulgaris)* bloom only in late summer, but they often have colorful foliage that becomes even more colorful in winter. Heaths *(Erica* sp.) bloom at various times; two indispensable species *(Erica × darleyensis* 'Silberschmelze' and *E. × d.* 'Darley Dale') bloom between November and April even in subfreezing temperatures. Planting in broad drifts gives ample opportunity to blend colors and extend blooming times. All species beg to be in the company of dwarf conifers, deciduous azaleas, spring bulbs, and ornamental grasses.

Wind, salt spray, and drenching November storms do not faze heaths and heathers; these plants are also drought tolerant (when established) in all but our hottest valleys. Plant them in the open, never under trees. Space them 3 feet/1 meter apart on average, giving vigorous or spreading forms more room, any dwarf forms less. Mulch to keep weeds down until plants fill in.

Young plants need watering until their fine but ultimately extensive roots get established. Being native to lean moor and mountain soils, they neither require nor like chemical fertilizer; however, a touch of liquid fish fertilizer is welcome.

Scotch heathers and summer-blooming heaths need a severe bowl haircut—below last year's flower spikes—every spring to prolong their life and keep them compact. Winter-blooming heaths need only a trim every two to three years, after blooming.

facing page Stone wall and rhododendrons provide a frame for *Calluna vulgaris* 'Robert Chapman', *Sedum* 'Autumn Joy', and two azaleas, *Rhododendron* 'Hino-crimson' and *R.* 'Hinodegiri', in the garden of Sherold Barr and John Kaib. above One of the finest winter heaths is *Erica × darleyensis* 'Darley Dale', which flanks the front walkway walk in Jennifer Aflatooni's front yard in Port Orchard, WA. It blooms throughout the winter. right *Calluna vulgaris* 'Robert Chapman' holds its golden-orange winter foliage color until spring. A strong upright grower, it is shown here against a contorted Harry Lauder's walking stick.

NORTHWEST ROCK GARDENS OFTEN FEATURE A WIDER RANGE OF NON-ALPINE
PLANTS THAN FOUND IN TRADITIONAL ENGLISH ROCK GARDENS.

rock
gardens

In midsummer, along the edges of high-mountain trails, exquisite plants produce delicate flowers that belie the harsh conditions in which they grew. Tucking themselves into the cracks of boulders, they form mounds in a sparkling array of subtle greens and grays. Many Northwest gardeners take their inspiration from these alpine scenes to design their backyard rockeries.

Our climate favors rock garden plants because even when days are hot, humidity is low, and nights are almost always cool. However, nurturing these plants, especially in the wetter parts of the Northwest, can be a challenge. Even with excellent drainage, some alpine plants cannot tolerate the continual winter moisture, or the lack of snow cover. The rocks most commonly used in these gardens are the natural basalt and granite stones that underlie much of the Northwest.

Any low-growing plant can be included if it does not scramble over slower-growing neighbors. A plant's origin can determine its suitability for your garden. Those from dry parts of Iran, Mexico, or Turkey, such as species tulips, thrive with southern Oregon's more limited rainfall. Alpine plants from China and the Himalayas, such as species delphiniums, can tolerate

At the front entry gate of Orin and Althea Soest's Sequim property is a sloping rock garden designed by Dan Hinkley. Sequim sits in a sunny microclimate that is ideal for a rock garden, and the mounds of soil ensure perfect drainage for the dwarf conifers, grasses, lewisias and other plants.

a wetter climate. But, in winter, Northwest rock gardeners still may find it necessary to put glass or plastic over vulnerable specimens.

Many garden perennials, such as geraniums, dianthus, and penstemons, have their miniature counterparts. Phlox, veronicas and a whole host of campanulas such as *Campanula cochlearifolia* and *C. carpatica* 'Blue Clips' and 'White Clips' are reliable performers. Small conifers and shrubs are welcome in the rock garden. The 4-inch/10-centimeter tall *Cotoneaster dammeri* 'Streib's Findling' (also known as *C. procumbens*) twines around the rocks with small white flowers and red berries.

top right Ground-hugging mounds of rocks and plants, connected with a pathway, create interesting groupings of texture and color. This collection includes phlox, *Daphne* 'Lawrence Crocker', mugho pine, and succulent *Cotyledon orbiculata*. bottom right A lupine native to Oregon, *Lupinus albifrons collinus*. below The rock garden of Phyllis and Dick Gustafson, of Central Point, Oregon, is based on a style developed in the Czech Republic and refined by Josef Halda. Rocks are placed in a tight pattern on a four-foot high mound, mimicking natural rock outcroppings. The crevices are planted with many plants, including *Lavandula angustifolia* 'Hidcote', *Verbascum dumulosum* 'Letitia', *Artemisia caucasica*, and a large *Agave parryi*.

THERE ARE TWO THINGS THAT BRING OUT THE BEAUTY IN A WINTER GARDEN: WHAT YOU PUT INTO IT, AND HOW YOU LOOK AT IT.

winter garden

What does winter mean to Northwest gardeners? Mii Tai who has been gardening in Spokane for over fifty years puts it this way, "There is a powerful serenity to it all. I look forward to the starkness of our maples against a gray winter sky and to the dry, tawny leaves and blooms of ornamental grass moving in an icy wind." Jerry McEwen in Anchorage loves the shadows and shapes in his garden on a long Alaskan winter night, "With a full moon on a carpet of snow, the garden is as brilliant at midnight as it is at high noon. There's a silvery magic to it." Doreen Plympton Strong in Portland likes to look out onto glistening stones and emerald mosses and the waxy leaves of rhododendrons, "It's like quietly slipping into bedrooms so you can watch your children deep in sleep."

Indeed, it is the subtle touches that will steal your heart. The elegance of raindrops beading-up on hellebore foliage. Sterling frost along the edges of sword ferns. The vivid trunks of the stewartias and birches and *Acer griseum*. Stepping-stones surrounded by a bed of lime green Scotch moss woven through with the sophisticated leaves of black mondo grass. And, perhaps most surprising, the way the naked branches of deciduous trees and shrubs like the Japanese maples, red- and yellow-twigged dogwoods, or even the ruddy branches of tree peonies become seasonal sculpture.

Just as in spring, summer, or autumn, you get out of the winter garden what you put into it. Leafless, deciduous plants become organic sculpture. Broad-leafed evergreens, ferns, and conifers bring a quiet gleam to dark corners. Textured or colored bark adds visual interest. Garden pattern and ornament become more dramatic. The bright fruits of cotoneaster, *Arbutus*

unedo, and mountain ash, and winter flowers like the reticulata irises or the pungently fragrant sarcococca don't drape the garden in color, they glitter sparingly like tastefully worn jewels.

If you've never cultivated a winter garden, start with a complete clean-up—raking, pruning, and cutting back—but leave handsome seedpods and dried flower heads in place. Look for places to create a view, or for voids and pockets of emptiness to fill. In all but the coldest parts of the Northwest, winter is a prime planting time. Add plants when weather allows, in the depth of the season or at the break of spring.

Remember, there's a place in most winter gardens for whimsy or a theatrical statement. Drain the birdbath and fill it with silver gazing balls in assorted sizes. Drape a statue with a garland of bay leaves or conifer sprigs. Surround the lion head mounted on the garden wall with white lights. Add a large glazed urn in red, yellow, or bright blue and fill it with a bouquet of pine boughs, bamboo shoots, photinia branches, and dogwood stems. Or hang an old mirror in a battered frame on a wall of ivy. With an investment of time, thought, and affection the winter garden can be as exuberant as an Arctic wind.

facing page A topiary garden shows off its strong structure when dusted by snow in this Bellingham garden. {LUNDQUIST GARDEN}
above A flowering cherry (*Prunus subhirtella* 'Eureka Weeping') displays its winter form. left top Bright red berries of *Cotoneaster franchetii* appear even more striking against a backdrop of dripping icicles. left bottom Drooping catkins of purple filbert dance in winter breezes. below Hazels are among the most valuable of Northwest winter garden plants. This Chinese witch hazel (*Hamamelis mollis*) is covered with intensely colored—and scented—flowers; the stems are great for cutting.

EXUBERANT GRASSES, WHETHER REACHING TO THE SKY OR CASCADING OVER THE
EDGE OF A PATH, BRING A SENSE OF MOVEMENT TO THE MOST SETTLED GARDEN.

ornamental
grasses

A graceful Japanese sweet flag (*Acorus gramineus* 'Ogon') lightly brushes these glass balls as they float on a pond in Val Easton's Seattle garden. The balls were blown using ash from the Mount St. Helens eruption.

Fifty years ago, when ornamental grasses were first introduced to the American gardening public, venturesome Northwest gardeners were among the first to incorporate them into their landscapes. This group of plants, which also includes sedges, flax, rushes, and other grasslike plants, can be found in every part of the Northwest. From the seaside to the mountains, by dry patches or bogs, and from sun to shade, there is a grass for any gardening situation.

Grasses make great plantings surrounding trees, accenting shrub borders, and accompanying perennials or spring bulbs, where their fast growth covers the bulbs' fading foliage. Many grasses bring the element of sound into the garden, rustling in the slightest breeze. Tall varieties like the 8-foot/2.5-meter *Miscanthus sinensis* add graceful height, and they can also be used to create a seasonal hedge. The tawny winter foliage and seed heads of certain grasses add structure to borders, standing up to rain or snow. Repeating a single type of grass in a bed can unify a disparate planting. Placed in drifts, grasses can appear to flow like water.

Easy-care grasses offer a wide variety of color even without flowers. The green-and-yellow-striped foliage of Japanese forest grass (*Hakonechloa macra* 'Aureola') glows in the shady border. Phormiums put out their swordlike leaves in colors ranging from deep red to vivid orange. The sedge *Carex elata* 'Aurea' softens the margins of ponds with its bright gold foliage, while the dark maroon leaves of annual fountain grass (*Pennisetum setaceum* 'Rubrum') add a touch of drama to any container planting.

When it comes to using grasses in the garden, Northwest gardeners are only limited by their imagination.

left Grasses make great pathside plantings; their silky flower heads are impossible for passersby to resist. This drought-tolerant planting includes Mexican feather grass *(Nassella tenuissima)* and, blooming in the background, blue fescue.

right A native combination suitable where garden blends into beach, yellow-flowered beach groundsel *(Senecio pseudoarnica)* blooms among driftwood, backed by blue lyme grass *(Elymus mollis)* and the darker backdrop of a Sitka spruce forest.

above New Zealand flax *(Phormium)* are among the best subjects for container plantings. These strappy grasslike plants shine, whether mixed into an exuberant blend or simply placed alone in a pot where they show off their multi-hued foliage.

LONG CONSIDERED EXOTIC OR INVASIVE, BAMBOOS ARE FINALLY FINDING THEIR
RIGHTFUL PLACE IN NORTHWEST GARDENS.

bamboo

Although only one species of bamboo is native to North America—and none to the Pacific Northwest—their ferny rustling foliage and swaying canes make these ancient plants seem at home in our gardens. Particularly useful as edgings or hedges, the taller bamboos also make striking specimens, adding drama and daring to the garden.

Running bamboos, such as most *Phyllostachys, Sasa,* and *Pleioblastus,* have given the family a bad reputation. Their strong rhizomes can find their way underneath sidewalks, into the foundation of your home, or out onto the street. Much better-behaved are their cousins, the "clumpers" (generally, those in the genus *Fargesia, Bambusa,* and *Chusquea)*. Although they too are rhizotamous, they send up shoots only a respectable distance from the center of the plant. Unless you have plenty of room to spare, stick with clumpers or slow runners.

Few bamboos are hardy in the coldest zones of the Northwest, although pushing down and covering the culms can get them through the winter. (The two *Fargesia* species listed at right are hardy to –20°F/–29°C.) But some bamboos, such as *Phyllostachys nigra,* grow better in our temperate climate than almost anywhere else on earth. Most bamboos require regular moisture, but they can't tolerate a boggy spot. All benefit from fertile, well-drained soil and a generous layer of mulch year round. Thin clumps regularly to allow sunlight to penetrate and to remove old culms and foliage. Clip smaller-diameter canes with pruners, but larger canes may call for a sharp saw. Remember that you can most likely find a use for the canes—as plant supports, fencing, or for decorative purposes.

Bamboos are particularly effective in containers, but their aggressive rhizomes can find their way out of the drainage holes in any pot that is placed on bare ground; slip a saucer under the pot to stop them.

above A stand of mixed black and green bamboo rises above a simple urn in Terry LeBlanc's garden. LeBlanc keeps the culms thinned, which gives the clump an airy, open look.

well-behaved bamboo

Alphonse Karr bamboo *Bambusa multiplex* 'Alphonse Karr'

Borinda fungosa

Umbrella bamboo *Fargesia murielae*

Fountain bamboo *F. nitida*

F.n. nymphenberg

Candy-stripe bamboo *Himalayacalamus falconori* 'Damarapa'

Phyllostachys bambusoides 'Castillon'

Black bamboo *P. nigra*

Yodake (metake) bamboo *Pseudosasa japonica*

Sasella masamuneana albostriata

Semiarundinaria fastuosa

Shibataea chinensis

Thamnocalamus tessellatas

above Even in winter, bamboo retains its strong character and color although it can sometimes use support under the weight of rain and snow. This grove of black bamboo *(Phyllostachys nigra)* underplanted with a Japanese aralia creates a forestlike screen beside the house.

right *Arundo donax* is a reed rather than a true bamboo, but its jointed stems and tall stature mean that it can serve similar landscape functions as its woody cousins. This variegated form *(A. d. variegata)* is shown here against a protected wall in a Salt Spring Island garden.

BIG-LEAFED PLANTS MAKE NORTHWEST GARDENS EXOTIC PLACES, WHERE PONDS
AND SHADY BORDERS BECOME SLICES OF JUNGLE, AND BOLD SHAPES SPICE UP THE
SIMPLEST PLANTINGS.

big-leafed plants

In the mild climates of the Pacific Northwest, a wide palette of big-leafed plants is available to add form and structure to gardens with enough water to quench their thirst.

To create the look of the sub-tropics, designers like Seattle-based Ben Hammontree mix bananas with gingers, giant ferns, ligularias, cannas, climbing roses, and honeysuckle, and even *Rhododendron macabeanum* (known for its enormous leaves). Portland garden designer Leslie Dotson added punch to her modest house with a pair of hardy bananas flanking the front entry. Dotson also likes gunnera, *Acanthus mollis,* cannas, and New Zealand flax, pairing them with more modest but equally exotic plants like snow gum *(Eucalyptus niphophila).*

Even if you aren't trying to re-create the tropics in your garden, there's good reason to add big-leafed plants. They are strong focal points, they break what can be the monotonous rhythm of our finely foliaged plants, and they stop the eye. Matched against a grand fern like *Osmunda regalis,*

a large-leafed hosta makes a strapping contrast. Try a hefty clump of blue *Hosta sieboldiana* 'Elegans' rising from a sweep of native ginger. Mix tall, big-leafed plants like hardy banana and Japanese aralia with native Douglas fir, cedar, and supple vine maples. The trick with these plants is to limb them up high and then plant a mix of big leaves and ferny foliage at ground level.

dinosaur dinner

Bear's breech *Acanthus mollis* Glossy green leaves are deeply lobed and up to 3 ft/1 m in length. Handsome bloom spikes can tower 5 ft/1.5 m. *A.m.* 'Latifolius' has larger leaves and is hardier.

Japanese aralia *Fatsia japonica* Fanlike leaves are 16 in./41 cm wide, leathery, and medium green in color. Plant grows 5 to 8 ft/1.5 to 2.5 m tall; remove lower leaves to show statuesque trunks. Spherical clusters of creamy white blooms become shiny black berries in winter.

Gunnera tinctoria The most prehistoric looking of the big-leafed plants. Deeply cut leaves can be 4 to 8 ft/1.2 to 2.5 m across on 4 to 6-ft/1.2 to 1.8-m stalks. Leaves are medium green, thick and rough textured. Bloom is like a huge, green corn cob. Needs lots of room and moisture.

Hosta 'Sum and Substance' This greenish-gold wonder has large, handsomely ribbed leaves (up to 2.5 ft/76 cm across).

Japanese banana *Musa basjoo* Can freeze to the ground in all but our very coldest climates and come back if given some protection at the base. The multi-stemmed plant grows to 15 ft/3 m tall, and has big leaves that last until a hard cold snap.

Japanese coltsfoot *Petasites japonicus* Giant perennial that must be placed with care; it can be invasive. Edible stalks are known as "fuki" in Japanese.

facing page The bog garden at Heronswood Nursery in Kingston evokes the Northwest's fog-enshrouded primeval forests. Hardy banana trees (*Musa basjoo*) introduce a steamy tropical note, and the gigantic coarse leaves of *Gunnera manicata* rising out of the bog appear to be a dinosaur's dinner in waiting. above Light shines through the arching umbrellalike leaves of gunnera, making striking patterns to contrast with the Oriental poppies below. {RISTOU GARDEN} right Hues in this dark-leafed banana (*Ensete ventricosum* 'Maurelii') echo the mature flower heads of statuesque cardoon (*Cynara cardunculus*). The flower heads can also be cut for dried arrangements.

THE NORTHWEST BOASTS SUCH A VARIED CLIMATE THAT BULBS FROM ALL OVER THE WORLD CAN FIND A HOME HERE.

bulbs

Bulbs (which include corms, rhizomes, and tubers) are temporary guests. From the delicate yellow blooms of the earliest winter aconites to the final carnival-colored show of dahlias, they come and go with the seasons. In areas with long cool springs, Northwest gardeners have the luxury of choosing next year's purchases by walking through huge commercial fields of blooming daffodils, tulips, lilies, or iris.

We also have a plethora of native bulbs, such as the nodding pale yellow bells of the fawn lily *(Erythronium oreganum)* or the glowing three-petaled trilliums, which accent spring woodlands. Many of these native bulbs have become the darlings of European breeders, and have returned to the Northwest in new guises and color. For instance, native camass *(Camassia quamash, C. cusickii,* and *C. leichtlinii),* which carpet moist meadows in spring, now sport names like 'Blauwe Donau' or 'Blue Danube', and they flower in shades of white and violet, as well as the common blue.

Instead of planting in clumps, sow bulbs in patterns, like ripples of water, flowing around trees, shrubs, and

above At the end of each bulb-selling season, Phyllis and Richard Null buy masses of Darwin hybrid tulips and plant them randomly throughout their Eugene garden. Each spring, the resulting patterns are wonderful surprises. right Asiatic lilies like these *Lilium* 'Milano', 'Peruga', and 'Cote d'Azur' are early bloomers. When planted in a group, they resemble a golden-headed shrub in full bloom, just when the rest of the garden is greening up after winter.

perennials, thus moving color around the garden. Early spring bulbs can thrive under deciduous trees before the leaves appear, and they are great companions around perennials whose expanding growth hides fading leaves. Larger bulbs are perfect for naturalizing grassy meadows and hillsides. Even water-wise gardens can feature spring-flowering bulbs like *Corydalis flexuosa* 'China Blue'. Summer-flowering varieties like crocosmia hybrids 'Jenny Bloom' or 'Lucifer' bring much-needed color to August gardens. Growing bulbs in pots allows you to display them at their peak, then remove them to let their foliage ripen offstage, and to keep the show coming season after season.

top right Small wooden bridges cross a vernal stream on this property, owned and landscaped by Marietta and Ernie O'Byrne. At the base of a stand of poplars is a wonderful mix of daffodils, bluebells (*Hyacinthoides non-scripta, H. hispanica*), hellebores, and knotweed. inset above The checkered reddish brown bells of *Fritillaria meleagris* are stunning in their detail. above A single daffodil sails above a sea of fawn lilies.

northwest native bulbs

Nodding onion *Allium cernuum*
Fire-cracker brodiaea *Brodiaea ida-maia*
Common camass *Camassia quamash*
Fairy bells *Disporum smithii*
Fawn lily *Erythronium sp.*
Fritillary *Fritillaria camschatcensis, F. recurva*
Crested iris *Iris cristata*
Tiger lily *Lilium columbianum*
Skunk cabbage *Lysichitum americanum*
Slink lily *Scoliopus hallii*
Blue-eyed grass *Sisyrinchium bellum*
False Solomon's seal *Smilacina racemose*
Western wake-robin *Trillium ovatum*
Corn lily *Veratrum viride*

left For late-summer bloom this combination of agapanthus and orange crocosmia was planted the previous spring. Statuesque perennials, such as bee balm *(Monarda)* and Cape fuchsia *(Phygelius)*, help add a last blast of color before fall. {HERONSWOOD NURSERY}

right Russet and brown tones are less-often used in borders, but can form pleasing combinations. Here, daylilies, golden yarrow, and reddish bronze leatherleaf sedge *(Carex buchananii)* combine shapes and colors in an easy-care early-summer garden.

left Rocketlike purple *Verbascum* and delphiniums, violet *Allium* balls, and flickering yellow *Geum* are like fireworks in a sky of green. Complementary colors (yellow/violet and red/green) make this Burnaby, B.C. scene even more explosive.

combinations

Seattle-based garden designers Glenn Withey and Charles Price have designed plantings that grace borders from The Bellevue Botanic Garden to private gardens throughout the Northwest and elsewhere. But they won't pretend that there is a magic formula for perfect borders. "A garden is always a process of give and take," says Withey. Some plants get eaten by deer or succumb to diseases; others explode with growth and crowd out their neighbors (case in point: *Cerinthe major* 'Purpurascens' that grew to the "size of a Volkswagen" and had to be removed). Still, we asked them to share with us a few tips for creating long-lasting, good-looking borders.

❧ DON'T GET HUNG UP ON FORMAL VERSUS INFORMAL. In the Beard garden, pictured above, formal lavender- and boxwood-edged parterres give the garden structure, which the designers then filled with more casual plantings. If you make the mistake of going too informal, you'll create a mishmash that will never soothe the eye.

❧ MAKE SURE THE BORDER IS GROUNDED WITH "ANCHOR" PLANTS that connect it to the earth. Anchors are generally compact plants, wider than they are tall.

❧ FOR A SOFTER LOOK, fill in the edges of the border with low, spreading plants that spill onto paths or lawns, such as dianthus, sunroses, verbena, or low-growing geraniums.

❧ THINK ARCHITECTURALLY. "We often work with a principle of domes and minarets," says Price. "A garden with contrasting round and upright shapes draws the eye to look around. A composition with all the same shapes is more restful, but we like excitement."

❧ PUNCTUATE THE PLANTING. Alliums are the ultimate exclamation points in a border; other choices include the taller *Agapanthus*, red-hot pokers, upright grasses, and conifers.

❧ DON'T OVERWHELM THE COMPOSITION. The tall *Ferula communis* above brings humor to the scene. But unlike a big-leafed plant, it's airy and transparent, so it's a pleasant surprise rather than an obvious sight gag.

❧ PLAN FOR LONGEVITY. Withey and Price use perennials that can grow back strongly when cut back through the season. They also favor tough customers like columbines and *Lathyrus vernus*. "You need plants that can tolerate being jostled by their neighbors," says Withey.

❧ THINK LONG-TERM. Choose plants that grow and bloom at different times. "Practice a little delayed gratification," urges Price, "otherwise the show is over while the season is still young."

THE BEST PERENNIAL PAIRINGS CONTRAST DIFFERENT SHAPES FOR DRAMA AND
REPEAT SIMILAR SHAPES TO ESTABLISH RHYTHM.

perennials

So many perennials grow well in the Northwest's inviting climate that it's tempting to grow everything, and end up with a mishmash. Resist! Picture your garden as a painting: Perennials with large flowers and colored leaves provide strong swathes of color, while plants with architectural form anchor the composition. Perennials with smaller flowers and subtler foliage compose the backdrop and frame, filling in the gaps and linking the star perennials to each other.

Tall, spiky flowers such as *Euphorbia characias wulfenii,* speedwells (*Veronica* hybrids), and delphiniums create an effect as strong as sculpture and contrast well with rounded or plate-shaped flower heads. Summer flowers—such as daylilies and summer phlox—bring round brush strokes of many colors to the border. Even in fall, the circular flowers of Japanese anemone or mauve Joe Pye weed make welcome splashes of color, combining well with most daisies.

left Showiest of all rounded flowers may be the ornamental onion Star of Persia *(Allium christophii)*. Here, in Thomas Hobbs's garden, it is combined with *Salvia verticillata*. below Among the daisies, best bets for the border are leopard's bane *(Doronicum cordatum)*, Shasta daisy, asters, coneflowers *(Echinacea)*, and rudbeckia. Shown here are *Echinacea purpurea* 'White Lustre' and *Aster* × *frikartii* 'Wonder of Staffa'.

below Trailing through this lush and cool green garden filled with edibles and perennials, you might be tempted to snap off a snow pea from the tepee, or stop by the umbrella-covered bench to admire the mixtures of soft blues, purples, and gold. Contributing to the tapestry are delphiniums, alliums, campanulas, *Echinops bannaticus*, and oakleaf hydrangea *(Hydrangea quercifolia)*. {FEENEY GARDEN}

facing page Flowers arranged in flat plates (usually clusters of small flowers packed tightly together) send dashes of horizontal color into the border. In this summer display, plates of rounded pink asters and red cannas, violet coneflowers, and yellow sneezeweed contrast with spiky purple fountain grass.

left Puffs of pink, violet, and bright green surround the silver foliage of this mounded cardoon in a lush perennial border. Next to the gray tones, other colors become almost fluorescent on hazy days.

The best flowers for creating clouds in the border are long-blooming and self-supporting. Mix colors, such as cerise *Gaura lindheimeri* 'Siskiyou Pink', yellow or misty lavender meadow rue (*Thalictrum flavum glaucum* or *T. delaveyi* 'Hewitt's Double') or frothy ivory *Artemisia lactiflora* 'Guizhou'.

It's easy to see through the veils created by loosely spaced stems, such as those created by the inflorescences of grasses or five-foot-tall *Verbena bonariensis*. Throughout the border, scatter flowers with long, flexible stems that can wind their way

above Staggered layers of grasses and perennials are set in a narrow bed against an evergreen background. Earth-toned cannas, dahlias, sneezeweed *(Helenium)*, and grasses make this a warm late-summer display.
left Set off such fiery shooting spears of red-hot poker *(Kniphofia uvaria)* by placing them against a darker background of green or bronze. Then fill around and in front with tumbling nasturtiums.

through the legs of other perennials. Best examples are cranesbills *(Geranium)* and *Potentilla atrosanguinea.*

Where a bed meets the lawn, frame the border with long-lasting edging plants. Pink *Geranium sanguineum striatum* is excellent, as is lavender, or canary-colored *Coreopsis verticillata* 'Moonbeam'.

Where the border meets pavement, edgers that billow are welcome. Along a walkway, enjoy drifts of 'Wisley Pink', red-orange 'Henfield Brilliant', and white 'St. Mary's' sun roses *(Helianthemum).* Let Santa Barbara daisy *(Erigeron karvinskianus)* fling pink and white flowers over the edge of a path. Gray-leafed *Sedum* 'Ruby Glow' and blue-green *S. sieboldii* drape foliage all summer, flowering pink in fall.

the gaps

In Des Kennedy's lighthearted look at our favorite pastime, *Crazy About Gardening,* he describes the sinking feeling that Northwest gardeners may experience come midsummer. That's when the fulsome glories of big, early perennials—the delphiniums, Oriental poppies, and all the rest—have faded away, leaving in their place the dreaded gaps. As he puts it, "Overnight, a great gaping hole opens up in the middle of everything; the entire composition falls hopelessly apart."

It takes a little creativity for gap-attacked gardeners to fill those eyesores. How do they do it?

❧ HAVE SOME ANNUALS READY. Sow them from seed earlier on in spring, or buy them in six packs at the local nursery. Favorites include alyssum, petunias, and snapdragons.

❧ PLUNK DOWN A GRASS OR TWO. Grasses are great fillers, sending up airy infloresences that take up a lot of space in a small amount of time. Fast-growers include purple fountain grass, *Calamagrostis* 'Karl Foerster', and switch grasses *(Panicums).*

❧ PLANT A POT. Or easier still, move one from the deck to the border. (The only drawback is the pots will need a twice-weekly watering at least; try drought-tolerant sempervivums.)

❧ ADD SOME ART. A sculpture, piece of driftwood, a pile of baskets painted blue, or even an empty urn can do wonders for a patch of cut-back perennial stems.

left In a shady garden, the blue-green puckered leaves of *Hosta sieboldiana* 'Elegans' peek through delicate greenery, which includes *Geranium × magnificum*. This simple planting can be enjoyed for up to five years or so, at which point the plants will need to be lifted and divided.

right Dramatic changes of texture and height can make even a small area look spacious. This corner planting includes relatively few flowers, but a great variety of foliage colors, shapes, and textures.

left A sunny, steep seaside garden needn't look sparse nor scrubby. Kathy Leishman, of Bowen Island, has found that such hardy perennials as Spanish lavender (*Lavandula stoechas*) and *Senecio greyi* combine well with *Sisyrinchium striatum* and hold their color even during drought periods.

noble geraniums

"I've been gardening this way for 70 years," says Phoebe Noble, "and now they call it the modern way." Well, proving that you can't argue with success, Noble's much-visited garden on Vancouver Island's Saanich Peninsula is both lush and lovely. "I like the garden to look like Mother Nature has designed it, not me," she says. Grass paths meander past overflowing borders, fruit trees are surrounded by greenery, and an extensive vegetable garden is tended by her daughter, Sandra Holloway.

How does she tend so much garden? By choosing plants that are easy to care for. "If they're a nuisance to themselves or their neighbors, they have to go," she declares. Fortunately, among her favorites (what she calls her "grand horticultural passion") are hardy geraniums, low-growing perennials whose delicate flowers and foliage belie their toughness. We asked her about them.

❧ FOR WEED-SUPPRESSING GROUND COVER and wilder parts of the garden, plant long-blooming *Geranium endressii* or *G.* × *oxonianum* (try 'Phoebe Noble', shown inset below). Mulch all plants heavily to conserve moisture and keep down weeds.

❧ IN THE PERENNIAL BORDER AND UNDER FRUIT TREES, try *G. macrorrhizum* ("When in doubt, plant *macrorrhizum*," says Noble). Many varieties have aromatic leaves that provide good fall color.

❧ IN SHADY SPOTS, try *G. phaeum,* either the maroon-flowered cultivars, or white-bloomed 'Album'.

❧ AS FOR CARE, Noble's advice is to leave the plants alone until they get leggy, then shear them to the ground. Noble herself uses a riding mower to cut back those in the front of the border. "A little water and they grow right back," she says happily.

ON ANY SUMMER DAY, LOCAL FARMERS MARKETS THROUGHOUT THE NORTHWEST OVERFLOW WITH AN INCREDIBLE BOUNTY OF FRESHLY PICKED FRUIT.

fruit

In the 1840s, when the first wagons ventured over the Oregon Trail, they carried young saplings of apples, plums, and pears, destined for the Willamette Valley. Since then, the Northwest has produced a wide variety of fruits and berries.

Apple, pear, plum, cherry, peach, and apricot trees are welcome additions to any garden design in the Northwest, where they add flowers, fall color, and winter form, as well as fruit. Many of the newest trees are smaller, like 'Alkemene' and 'William's Pride' apples, which stay in the 12- to 15-foot/4- to 5-meter range without pruning. Dwarf trees grow 4 to 6 feet/1 to 2 meters, perfect for small backyards, and columnar apples take up even less space.

The hardy kiwi (*Actinidia arguta*) is becoming a popular vine in home gardens. The green fruit is smooth-skinned and more flavorful than the kind sold in stores. The handsome vines can attain 30 feet/9 meters, and need to be trained to a sturdy fence or arbor.

Native plants like elderberry (*Sambucus caerulea*), thimbleberry (*Rubus parviflorus*), and salmonberry (*Rubus spectabilis*) are all easy-care shrubs that tolerate partial shade. They are an excellent choice for water-wise gardens.

above Ideal for edible gardens with small spaces, a colonnade of 'Northpole' apples fit snugly into Elizabeth Lair's Oregon garden. These specially-bred trees form fruit on short spurs that develop along the main trunk. right Looking out from underneath a canopy of hardy kiwi over beds of edible ornamentals at Sooke Harbour House in B.C.

Garden enclosures Espalier trees or Belgian fences of apple, plum, cherry, or pear.

Shady arbors Smother them with hardy kiwi, golden hops (*Humulus lupulus* 'Aureus') or grapes.

Edible groundcovers *Arctostaphylos uva-ursi* 'Massachusetts', bunchberry (*Cornus canadensis*), strawberries, groundcover raspberry (*Rubus*), lingonberry (*Vaccinium vitus-idaea minus*).

Hedges Edge the garden with hazelnut (*Corylus* sp.), currants, native elderberry (*Sambucus mexicana*), highbush blueberries, or cranberries.

Small accents Try these trees in the border: pawpaw (*Asimina triloba*), dwarf crabapple 'Tina', mulberry (*Morus*), dwarf cherry 'Compact Stella'.

Border fruit Mix in with other perennials: serviceberry, black chokeberry (*Aronia melanocarpa*), currants, goumi (*Elaeagnus multiflora*), Himalayan honeysuckle (*Leycesteria formosa*), and gooseberry (*Ribes sp.*).

Many parts of the Northwest lie on the same parallel as the great grape-growing regions of France and Germany. The past 50 years have seen a tremendous rise in the number of wineries in Oregon, Washington, and British Columbia, and many varieties of table grapes are now grown. The hotter summer regions favor all grapes, but vines like 'Canadice', 'Glenora', and classic 'Interlaken' ripen best in the cooler summers of the maritime Northwest. Grow grapes on a fence or slope, especially facing south or west, or on overhead supports. The ubiquitous Douglas fir peeler poles make a classic Northwest-style arbor.

above and inset Mary-Kate Mackay has a bounty of grapes in her Eugene garden, starting in mid-August, when the first of her four grape varieties starts to ripen. 'Himrod' is followed by 'Lakemont', 'Flame', and then 'Concord'. When the grapes are dormant in January, she prunes back each vine to its own quadrant on top of the arbor; by June, the entire structure is smothered with foliage and ripening fruit.

SELECT ROSES TO FIT PARTICULAR PLACES AND PURPOSES: FOR THE FRONT, MIDDLE, OR BACK OF A BORDER; TO CLIMB OVERHEAD; OR TO COVER THE GROUND.

roses

Some roses do spectacularly well in the Northwest; others fail miserably, growing leggy, sparse, and flowerless. Fortunately, our love affair with these gorgeous plants keeps us seeking varieties that are graceful in shape, disease resistant, and good companions for perennials and annuals. For inside information on the best roses for your area, contact one of the Northwest's many rose societies. Here are a few rose choices to get you started.

For the border's edge, try 'The Fairy', 'Lovely Fairy', or single-flowering 'Minilights'. Two compact, fragrant rugosas are single pink 'Frau Dagmar Hartopp' and semidouble violet 'Purple Pavement'.

Roses with billowing flower clusters, such as 'Bonica', mix well with perennials. Many wide-spreading hybrid musk roses—'Cornelia', 'Ballerina', 'Red Ballerina', 'Lavender Lassie', 'Mozart', 'Danae', 'Penelope', and 'Prosperity'—also blend well in midborder. For the back of the border, try tall *Rosa moyesii* and its near hybrids, 'Sealing Wax', 'Geranium', and 'Highdownensis'.

Rugosa hybrids form dense, thorny thickets good for barrier hedges and bird habitat. Sumptuous 'Westerland', with its fragrant, double apricot flowers that cut well for bouquets; pink-and-cream 'New Face'; and vivid pink 'Lyric' all make outstanding screens or back-of-the-border specimens.

Groundcover roses should be low-growing, dense enough to smother weeds, and bloom well. 'Carefree Delight', 'Eyeopener', and the Flower Carpet series are outstanding.

facing page, inset Bourbon rose 'La Reine Victoria' *facing page, bottom* A cottage garden is the perfect setting to show off the appeal of roses. A gate with a mossy wreath opens up to an arbor cloaked with 'Natchitoches Noisette' and 'Pink Mermaid'. Just to the side of the brick walk are 'Albertine' roses, surrounded by delphinium, peonies, and hibiscus.

above Pink 'Gertrude Jekyll', clambers over a trellis and spills out over the sides in a mass of deep pink, fragrant blossoms. Old-fashioned phlox echoes the abundance of the rose. *right Rosa* 'Dortmund' produces crimson flowers on thorny stems; it's happiest in a casual setting such as here, poking through a deep blue fence.

art

DECOR · DUANE KELLY · LIGHT
CONTAINERS · CONTAINER SECRETS
WATER · BIRDS · NATURAL · BONSAI
SALVAGE · FURNITURE · STRUCTURES

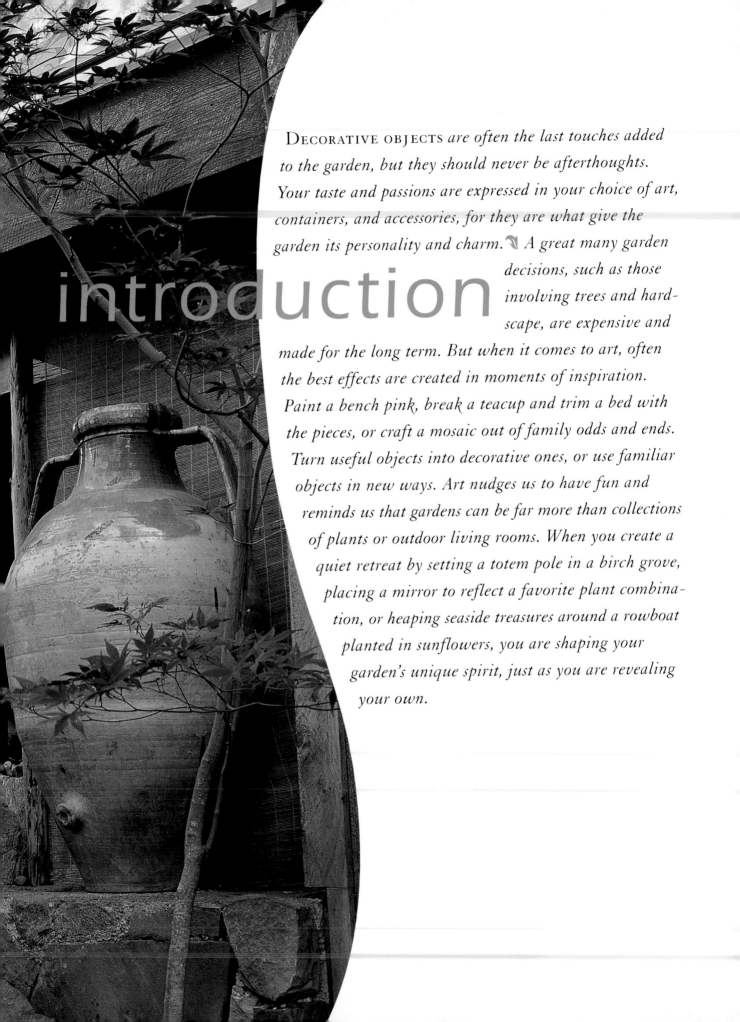

DECORATIVE OBJECTS *are often the last touches added to the garden, but they should never be afterthoughts. Your taste and passions are expressed in your choice of art, containers, and accessories, for they are what give the garden its personality and charm.* ❧ *A great many garden decisions, such as those involving trees and hardscape, are expensive and made for the long term. But when it comes to art, often the best effects are created in moments of inspiration. Paint a bench pink, break a teacup and trim a bed with the pieces, or craft a mosaic out of family odds and ends. Turn useful objects into decorative ones, or use familiar objects in new ways. Art nudges us to have fun and reminds us that gardens can be far more than collections of plants or outdoor living rooms. When you create a quiet retreat by setting a totem pole in a birch grove, placing a mirror to reflect a favorite plant combination, or heaping seaside treasures around a rowboat planted in sunflowers, you are shaping your garden's unique spirit, just as you are revealing your own.*

introduction

ART IN THE GARDEN CAN MEAN ANYTHING FROM SAUCERS OF BEACH
GLASS TO STATUESQUE SCULPTURES. THE EFFECTIVENESS OF ANY PIECE
LIES NOT IN ITS VALUE BUT IN HOW YOU USE IT.

decor

When you select important pieces of art, make sure they
harmonize with the style of your home and garden, any
existing materials, and perhaps most of all, the size and scale of
your property. Outsized pots or underscale furniture can lend
distinction, surprise, or humor, but such objects must be carefully
placed or they will be overwhelming—or worse, insignificant.
Statues can be prominently displayed as focal points, or for a less
formal look, you can integrate them with plantings. Above all,
feel free to place art at all levels of the garden: mosaics underfoot,
sculptures reflected in wall mirrors, or ornate overhead arches
that cast intriguing shadows along the garden path.

facing page Statuary links the house with its surroundings. A hefty Italian olive oil jar, flanked by
stout support timbers and framed by the laciness of a Japanese maple, fills a niche in the garden of
wildlife artist Robert Bateman's home on Salt Spring Island in British Columbia. above In this marriage
of the valuable with the commonplace, hollyhocks, foxgloves, and leeks in a Whidbey Island garden
surround a voluptuously curved Dante Marioni vase. {JOHANNA NITZKE MARQUIS GARDEN}

right Metal, stone, and leaf have a natural affinity, as shown by an outsized ladybug sculpture, crafted by Kelli Ellen. In this Shelton, Washington, garden, the sheen of its mottled back sets off the roughness of a granite slab and the arch of daylily foliage. below The focal point of this potager is a vegetable washing basin in the shape of a chanterelle mushroom. Bluestone pavers are softened by a fluff of feather grass (Nassella tenuissima) tall oxblood-red pots, and a cluster of concrete spheres. Basin and spheres by Little and Lewis. {HERONSWOOD NURSERY, KINGSTON, WA}

above, top Perched on a rusted metal stand, the patterns of tile and stone on this handmade mosaic ball catch the light—and your attention. above, bottom This contemporary take on a totem pole, called Balancing Act, was once part of a 100-year-old cedar tree that blew down in a severe Vashon Island winter storm. Thanks to artist Bill Dilley, the tree now graces the garden in a new form.

A perennial border is effectively punctuated with the addition of a simple wooden tower, painted blue-gray to blend with the burgundy, pink, and silvery shades of flowers and foliage. The tower's peaked top leads the eye to the view of salt water beyond.
{JENNIFER WALL GARDEN, LUMMI ISLAND, WA}

left A plump, oversize, ruby-red pomegranate, made by artists George Little and David Lewis, has the place of honor atop a pedestal in a tropical-esque Bainbridge Island garden. below Pretty pink ornamental oregano (*Origanum laevigatum* 'Hopley's Purple'), 'Southern Charm' verbascum, and purple coneflower make a charming surround for a metal flower sculpture that seems to spring from the ground along with the plants. facing page This six-foot steel and hammered copper sculpture, made by sculptor Lee Proctor, weaves its way toward the sky in this mountain garden owned by Chris Moritz.

duane kelly

knows about garden art: After all, he's seen plenty of it during his years as producer of the Northwest Flower and Garden Show. Every February, he and his staff assemble designers from across the Northwest and beyond to build display gardens that bring together plants and art.

Some of the gardens represent high drama — theater, really. Colored lights play across pools lined with bits of colored recycled glass, for example, or cast a moody red glow upon tall, ancient-looking, stone pillars bursting with tropical plants. Others show slices of mossy, moist Northwest forest at its most idyllic, in which natural elements like stone and weathered, gnarled branches accent burbling streams edged with ferns and conifers. The show is fertile ground for all sorts of creative ideas that inspire — and stretch the thinking of — those who visit.

In Kelly's own garden in Ballard, classical accents nestle among plants. "I'm a student of the Roman garden," he explains. "I have a bust of Hermes, a bust of Apollo, and a birdbath decorated with the Three Graces. This leap across the millennia gives me pleasure. It adds another level of meaning to my garden.

"Some gardeners like modern or abstract art," he adds. "Others like loud color. Some just want to do it all with plants. Find what resonates for you."

Beyond that, celebrate what nature provides. "A garden is one of the most important sources of beauty on our planet," says Kelly. "It's a great art form. It changes with time, looking different tomorrow than today. It dies in winter, and is reborn anew each spring. Those cycles are an important source of its beauty."

THE FLICK OF A SWITCH OR THE STRIKE OF A MATCH CAN RECAPTURE PATHS, PONDS, AND PLANTINGS FROM THE DARKNESS, ESPECIALLY ON WINTER EVENINGS. THE RESULT IS YEAR-ROUND WARMTH.

light

When the weather is cold or wet, spotlight your garden so that you can enjoy it from indoors, nose against the windowpane. There are three basic effects: *backlighting,* which throws the subject into silhouette; *down-lighting,* to give a subtle feel of natural light; and *uplighting,* which reverses the natural direction of light, shining through branches and structures, creating dramatic shadow play.

Lighting options range from high-tech spotlights to simple candles. Low-voltage lighting is inexpensive, and sold in do-it-yourself kits. Fiber optics pipe light from a central source through fibers no thicker than a strand of hair. Lanterns—electric and candlelit—gleam on tabletops or hang from trees. Strings of festive holiday lights glow like tiny stars when wrapped around tree trunks, or trimming for the edge of a garden umbrella. Most romantic of all is candlelight, which no garden should be without. Try floating candles in dishes of water, filling an old chandelier with votives, or setting a row of tiki torches along a path.

A beautiful focal point by day or night, this cast-concrete winged Nike graces the garden of Robyn Coleman in Seattle. To steer the eye towards the statue, Coleman designed a modified knot garden of dwarf boxwood twining around pink astilbe. At night, Nike is softly illuminated with a spotlight.

right Gracefully holding aloft her candelabra, this sculptured figure appears to cast a tender gaze downward. Come evening, the combination of flickering candlelight, the classical allusion, and a surround of fragrant lilies is eternally romantic. below Wall sconces that look good by night or day, such as this one designed by Judith Jones, are made even more compelling by the trails of ivy that creep up and around.

left As night falls, handmade lanterns brighten the covered deck of Les Brake's home in Willow, Alaska. Brake lightly sprays the inside of a mold such as a plastic bucket with vegetable oil, then he fills it with water. When ice forms around the sides and bottom of the mold, he pours out the unfrozen water to leave a cylinder of ice. Inverted, with a candle placed inside, the lantern makes a frosty shimmer of warmth.

CONTAINERS MAY BE THE ULTIMATE GARDEN ACCESSORIES — THE PERFECT
VEHICLES FOR INDIVIDUAL EXPRESSION. IN FACT, FOR MANY URBAN
DWELLERS THE CONTAINERS ARE THE GARDEN.

containers

Pots can be coordinated by color, style, or texture, or you can collect as wide a variety of pots as you do vases for interior arrangements. Mix classic terra-cotta urns with glossy aqua or burgundy pots; or pair sophisticated matte black with brightly painted wooden planter boxes. Outfit urban rooftops and terraces with smooth metal planters, and trim houseboats with window boxes. Then move and change your containers with the seasons, or your whims.

An elegant and easy trick is to place just one kind of plant in each pot, and then rearrange the pots to suit your fancy. Don't confine your-self to flowering plants—put anything in pots you wish to emphasize or protect. Go beyond familiar combi-nations of annuals and stuff a cobalt blue urn with yellow cherry tomatoes or plant a washed-green wooden container with copper-colored bougainvillea. Architectural plants such as phormiums or agaves, and lush foliage plants such as coleus or *Helichrysum,* look their best in containers. As with all good design, the key to success lies in combination, repetition, emphasis, and pleasing your own eye.

Words draw the eye and encourage us to slow down, read, and remember. A glossy pot calls attention to an aged piece of wood inscribed with a Greek philosopher's thoughts on the blessings of owning a simple piece of property. {MARK HENRY GARDEN, SNOHOMISH, WA}

top left By combining a tall, blue-glazed ceramic urn with a similarly toned hosta, this dark corner has been turned into a focal point. Plant and pot relate to each other perfectly because both have sufficient height and heft to fill in the corner, while the ribbed splay of the hosta leaves echo the rounded shape of the urn. **top right** Unplanted pots work as statuary nestled into beds and borders. The rough texture, generous bulge, and pale coloration of this urn is a perfect foil to the deep red, spiky burst of barberry behind it. The pot lightens up the whole composition, accenting the white flowers and silver foliage that cool down the predominant tones of maroon and magenta. **bottom left** Set in a small-space garden designed by Michael Luco, a multi-graft apple tree is surrounded purple petunias. **bottom right** In this profuse poolside arrangement (one of twenty-five), Juanita Nye started by placing a *Phormium* at the top and surrounded it with coral and fuchsia colored bougainvillea, willow, salvia, *Vinca major* 'Variegata', curly-leaf parsley, *Achillea millefolium* 'Fire King', *Hibiscus rosasinensis* 'Fire Wagon', and bee balm.

top left This large and diverse group of plants share similar water and sun needs. The layered combination includes *Nandina*, *Abutilon pictum* 'Gold Dust', nicotiana, *Artemisia* 'Powis Castle', French marigolds, and ice plant. {JUANITA NYE DESIGN} above A diversity of pots and plants creates a stylish mix of varying heights and shapes. Pots can be rearranged throughout the season to emphasize whatever is looking best at the moment and to accent plants in the nearby border. {VALERIE MURRAY GARDEN, VICTORIA}. left The sweetness of spring pansies is spiced up by spiky *Cordyline australis* 'Albertii' and a terra cotta pot packed with flamboyant *Tulipa* 'Marjolien'. The tulips have such impact because they are grouped in a pot and raised above the surrounding foliage. {MILLER BOTANICAL GARDEN, SEATTLE} facing page Stephanie Feeney created this classical vignette in Bellingham by artfully filling two large pots with red petunias and violet verbena and setting them on a staging area of ivy-covered stone.

top left This large and diverse group of plants share similar water and sun needs. The layered combination includes *Nandina, Abutilon pictum* 'Gold Dust', nicotiana, *Artemisia* 'Powis Castle', French marigolds, and ice plant. {JUANITA NYE DESIGN} above A diversity of pots and plants creates a stylish mix of varying heights and shapes. Pots can be rearranged throughout the season to emphasize whatever is looking best at the moment and to accent plants in the nearby border. {VALERIE MURRAY GARDEN, VICTORIA}. left The sweetness of spring pansies is spiced up by spiky *Cordyline australis* 'Albertii' and a terra cotta pot packed with flamboyant *Tulipa* 'Marjolien'. The tulips have such impact because they are grouped in a pot and raised above the surrounding foliage.{MILLER BOTANICAL GARDEN, SEATTLE} facing page Stephanie Feeney created this classical vignette in Bellingham by artfully filling two large pots with red petunias and violet verbena and setting them on a staging area of ivy-covered stone.

container secrets

Is it a stretch to jam 13 plants into a 24-in/60-cm container? Not for Tina Dixon, whose Plants à la Carte design firm, based in Bothell, Washington, specializes in such things. "Someone asked me once which rules I break most. Spacing's one of them," she says. "I pack the plants in."

Dixon's secrets?

❧ USE COLOR ECHOES. The dark eye of a black-eyed Susan vine might echo the color of a dark-leafed sweet potato vine, just as purple fountain grass might pick up the hue of chocolate cosmos.

❧ ADD TEXTURED BACKDROPS FOR FLOWERS—a pair of bronze fennel plants fluffing out behind a 'Goldsturm' black-eyed Susan, for instance.

❧ BALANCE YOUR COMPOSITION for color and texture. Set an upright, red-foliaged plant in back and a red-foliaged trailer at the front, with green and gold or gray foliage between. If you put a wispy upright plant behind a bold trailer your composition will look bottom-heavy.

❧ USE LARGE POTS, at least 20 in/50 cm in diameter. Dixon favors plastic containers made to look like stone or terra-cotta, Asian pottery ("great colors and shapes"), and concrete or stone.

Dixon starts planting summer pots on May 1 (those closest to Puget Sound, where weather is mildest, are planted first). She uses commercial potting soil fortified with slow-release fertilizer (such as 14–14–14), waters the pots daily (twice a day in hot weather), and deadheads throughout the season to keep plants blooming. Closely spaced plants are heavy feeders, so she applies a liquid fertilizer every two weeks. At the end of September, she replaces summer bloomers with fall ones, and tucks in bulbs for bloom the following spring.

WATER IS AS ESSENTIAL TO A GARDEN AS ARE PLANTS. ALL THE GARDEN'S INHABITANTS, BOTH HUMAN AND NATIVE, ARE IRRESISTIBLY DRAWN TO IT.

water

Water captured and contained draws us in to look for a flash of fish scales, a reflection of the sky, or the ripple of wind across its surface. Even a dish of still water reflects the passing clouds and swaying trees, and is a magnet for birds, dragonflies, and insects. Place plucked blossoms or colored glass balls in the water to add more movement.

In the muddy shores of even a small pond you can find frogs, water skippers, and butterflies "puddling" their wings in the mud. But it is moving water that casts a spell of enchantment, with its rushing and rhythmic dripping. Waterfalls, fountains, and watercourses all provide both motion and music. Orchestrate these by adding stones for water to tumble around, or by using a small recirculating pump.

above Towering evergreens are reflected in the smooth surface of the pond in the Waterman garden on Bainbridge Island. Water drips from the folds of a concrete *Gunnera* leaf, and "floating" across the pond are a series of stepping-stones. left Nestled into foliage and surrounded by similarly hued flowers, this little bamboo-spout fountain is perfectly integrated into its spot.

left, top Glazed pottery balls appear as crinkled and curious as dinosaur eggs when covered by water and grouped in a sculpted granite bowl. Set atop a driftwood stump surrounded by beach stones, the arrangement has the feel of treasures found on a Northwest salt-water beach. left A foggy mist rises from the surface of a rushing streambed. The water, lit from beneath, takes on a translucent quality as it flows around a blend of dark and light foliage plants and ornamental grasses. above, top Every body of water captured in the garden, whether simple dishrock or grandiose pond, reflects the sky above, passing clouds, and nearby plantings. Here a low bowl of water reflects a delicate pot of pale pansies secured in a free-standing metal frame. above Stepping-stones that lead to a shallow pond in Barbara Flynn's garden contain a message for those who take time to observe.

above This stair-step watercourse was constructed of humble cement block, allowing water to flow down the hill between a knot garden and a collection of dramatic perennials.

right, top Despite its typically challenging northwestern topography, this steep hillside was turned into a garden with a series of stone walls, rocky streambeds, waterfalls, plantings, and small ponds. The cascading foliage of a Japanese maple echoes the flow of the nearby waterfall.

right, center A clever way to direct moisture to plants under the eaves is to run a rain chain from the roof. This one, in Rick Graham's Hornby Island garden, is nicely balanced between two windows. far right Large boulders and lush greenery disguise a former hot tub in Cindy and Steve Stockett's Vashon Island garden.

Ponds inspire different types of reflection. Part of a larger water garden on Mercer Island, the concrete shell of this koi pond was sealed with black epoxy paint; this dark finish gives the water a mirrorlike quality. A standing granite monolith sculpture is hefty enough to balance the scale of the substantial deck and arbor—especially important under an open sky.

This sleek birdbath provides both the still, shallow water birds need to bathe, and an arched jet of water for sound and splash.

THE GARDEN IS RICHER FOR THE SONGS OF BIRDS AND THE FLASH OF THEIR WINGS, BUT WE MUST DO OUR PART TO ATTRACT THEM. FORTUNATELY, THERE ARE MANY WAYS TO DO SO.

birds

A wide variety of shrubs, trees, and flowers provide food, shelter, and nesting materials for birds. For the most enticing garden, create a natural habitat by mimicking the layers of a Northwest forest and including native plants, some with berries, others with nectar-rich blooms.

Birds will splash happily in any shallow vessel that holds water. Running water is also attractive to birds—as well as to dragonflies, butterflies, and bees. Hang birdhouses from trees or place them atop fence posts, away from predators, so that birds can set up housekeeping. Feeders can be both beautiful and practical, whether you purchase a glimmering, blown-glass hummingbird feeder or find a natural depression in a pond-side boulder to fill with sunflower seeds.

right Birdhouses not only provide homes and shelter, but also add height and embellishment. Plastic pears and curly wrought iron finials tart up a birdhouse in a garden near Nanaimo on Vancouver Island. {GRANT LEIER/NIXIE BARTON GARDEN}

above Moss softens a concrete birdbath in a shady, sheltered corner of this garden. right This Mission, B.C., birdhouse becomes art with shaggy sedums forming its roof and base, and a planted shoe on the post. Sedums are a good choice for such flourishes, for they require little soil or water to look good year-round. far right Birdbaths are best integrated in with garden plants so that birds have both cover and food close by. In this naturalistic garden in Victoria, a leaf-shaped birdbath is surrounded with perennials such as crocosmia and ligularia, which provide colorful, leafy shade and shelter.

OBJECTS BORN OF WIND AND WEATHER, TIDES AND FOREST HAVE AN INTRINSIC
AFFINITY FOR EACH OTHER. THAT'S WHY IT'S SO EASY TO FIT THEM INTO OUR
LUSH NORTHWEST GARDENS.

natural

Choosing natural objects, such as stones, shells, or weathered
wood, is a foolproof way to personalize the garden. Stumps
left in place become vertical accents grown mossy with age. Outdoor tables
can be dressed up with platters of agates that turn saltwater shiny in the
rain. Stone becomes Japanese-style sculpture when you place a single large
boulder by an aged pine. The tree, in turn, can be pruned to complement
the boulder's curvaceous shape. And as a bonus, collecting such objects for
your garden inspires hikes in the mountains, walks on the beach, and a
desire to reflect in the garden the beauty of the world around us.

The Kruckeberg Botanic Garden in Shoreline, Washington, is known for its extensive native plant collection beneath a canopy of old-growth firs. A metal Indian, found buried on the property many years
ago, peeks humorously from a stump filigreed with the lacy foliage of a cut leaf maple (Acer palmatum).

left A gathering of objects is more effective than a few things strewn about. This stone bowl full of Bellingham Bay beach rocks adds to the mythic feel of a structure with a Navaho breastplate design. Scale is always trickiest outdoors under the vastness of the open sky, and the fat timbers of the arbor, and the heft of bowl and stones are in perfect proportion.

above, right Ferns line a pathway of mortared river cobbles. On drizzly days, the rain-slicked surface takes on the luminosity of a Northwest stream. {KEITH GELLER DESIGN} above Nature offers a stone bench for seating; the human touch is added by setting it on short wooden pillars and etching its surface. Such furniture crafted of natural materials blends seamlessly into this Kitsap Peninsula garden. {ELANDAN GARDENS, DIANA AND DAN ROBINSON} left Framing for emphasis is as important in the garden as inside the house; the eye is drawn to that which is enclosed. The window in this fence in Willow, Alaska, shows off a collection of delphiniums and other perennials within. {LES BRAKE DESIGN}.

bonsai

is living art, long associated with Asian gardens, where the techniques of training trees into miniature form originated. Traditional forms of indoor display include special alcoves called "Tokonoma" or wooden stands known as "Shoku." Outdoors, the placement of bonsai should be considered just as carefully. After all, bonsai plants are often more venerable than their mature counterparts in the garden.

Here are some guidelines for displaying bonsai

❧ ELEVATE the tree as close to eye level as possible so its form can be appreciated.

❧ BONSAI are always grown in shallow containers to restrict their roots. But you can place the pot on a shelf, piece of driftwood, boulder, or upturned urn, as shown here in Terry Welch's garden in Woodinville.

❧ CASCADING bonsai branches should not touch the surface on which they are placed. Traditionally, cascading bonsai are placed in the center of their pot, whereas upright trees are placed off center.

❧ SIMPLICITY is key in bonsai aesthetics. Display prized specimens alone, against an uncluttered background, such as a simple wall or fence. Accents in the display should be appropriate to the setting; typical are artifacts such as stones, scrolls, or miniature bridges or temples.

salvage

ITEMS WITH AN OBVIOUS PAST BRING A SENSE OF STORY-TELLING TO THE GARDEN. AND LIKE STORIES, THEY CONTAIN ELEMENTS OF HUMOR, HISTORY, AND CURIOSITY.

A mellow patina on a fence or garden bench lends an air of elegance and comfort, much like the effect of an antique in a living room. And although rusty metal may be unwelcome elsewhere, it complements all the greens of nature. You can do the environment—and your wallet—a good turn by choosing recycled materials such as glass tiles, salvaged objects, used bowling balls, or antique metal gates. The trick is to look at familiar objects in creative new ways. An old wooden-frame window can find new life when hung from an arbor; aged tools can be painted brightly or inlaid with mosaics and hung on the garden shed; '50s-era theater seats or metal dress-maker's dummies can be parked in borders to support floppy plants. Local public-utility companies often supply information on recycled products for the garden. To bring a bit of Northwest history into your garden, peruse garage sales, antique stores, and architectural salvage centers for reusable—and unusual—objects.

above, left Discarded machinery seems to have sprouted overnight like toadstools in this Oregon garden. Salvaged rusty metal is a perfect material for the Northwest, for it looks as though it has weathered many a wet winter. {RICHARDS/PIEKOW GARDEN} above, right A long, leafy driveway on Whidbey Island curves to reveal a towering pyramid of bowling balls. The garden's owner used to scatter the balls around the garden, but ended up with so many she built this solid pyramid at its entrance. The plain balls are on the inside, with the patterned ones revealed as colorful counterpoint to the green of ferns and trees. {JOHANNA NITZKE MARQUIS GARDEN}

top Mirrors expand space and multiply plants, creating a little pleasant directional confusion. An elongated oval mirror, mounted onto a fence in this Denman Island, B.C., garden reflects a cluster of perennials, doubling their color and leafiness. {DES AND SANDY KENNEDY GARDEN} above An old fence section divides this Portland garden and displays a disparate group of found objects. Pots, rusty hinges, and a croquet mallet form a whimsical still life. The interlacing of vines ties the manmade grouping to the garden and fills in the gaps for more effective screening. {NANCY GOLDMAN GARDEN} left Peeling white paint and windowpanes are a recipe for nostalgia, as is a pale pink climbing rose, which drapes its old-fashioned flowers over this arbor. The window is hung from a crosspiece with chains, providing views of the garden from both indoors and outdoors at once.

furniture

Durability and sturdiness are vital criteria for outdoor furniture that will be exposed to the elements. Comfort is equally important, for only when you are relaxed can you take proper note of butterflies, stars, or a lily's perfume.

Place chairs and benches in far corners to lure guests out into the garden; nothing is more tempting than a bench glimpsed around a corner of the path, a brightly striped hammock strung between two trees, or little chairs and a private tea table tucked into a sunny spot.

Twiggy rattan evokes the Northwest's many island gardens. Sleek aluminum or stainless steel is a perfect match for urban courtyards and balconies. Cedar and teak pieces are classics. Furniture affords you the chance to move your interior style out into the garden. If you have a covered porch or patio, move an overstuffed chair outside for the summer, or create a practical focal point by painting a simple wooden chair chartreuse or periwinkle blue.

A distant view of intensely blue water reminds you that this is an island, while the peeled pole arbor delineates a gravel terrace that is conveniently close to the house yet planted and framed so as to feel quite separate. As vines grow up to cover the arbor, they'll provide shelter from the prevailing sea winds, a necessity on Vashon Island. {LINDA WEISS DESIGN}

left, top A simple bench matches the Asian elegance of this Woodinville garden. Its mottled surface speaks of turbulent Northwest winters, yet it invites you to sit and watch the beaver at work in the pond or the flight of herons overhead. {TERRY WELCH GARDEN}

left Stylish seating needn't be store-bought or familiar. The curved shape and pebbly surface of a mosaic chair resembles a turtle's shell, introducing humor into this Victoria garden as it lightens a shady nook beneath a pruned-up camellia. {VALERIE MURRAY GARDEN}

above Weather-worn by nature and stained by hand, the driftwood for this simple chair was gathered on the beaches of Denman Island, B.C.

left What says cozy more than plump cushions and an afghan? Set off by a woven fence, arbor, and a thicket of tall plantings, the red wicker settee and coffee table offer a secluded respite. The effect of a separate room is emphasized by the potted geraniums that relate in color and scale to the furniture rather than to the surrounding garden.

below Make seating a part of the garden by choosing furniture pieces that exude history. This faded bench in a Portland garden looks as if it's been weathering away for generations. The bench seems rooted into the garden, an illusion created by flanking it with pots overflowing with the dark leaves and explosive blooms of *Ligularia* 'Othello'. {GOLDMAN GARDEN}

left The craftsmanship of this handmade bench makes it both a destination and an object of art. An Asian flair in the design fits in beautifully with the hushed surroundings, while the gently arched roof and curving seat back are reminiscent of the nearby ocean. below Modern furniture that matches the style of this island home carries the sleek, contemporary theme out into the garden. Glass doors open to a terrace topped with a narrow arbor and a slab for an outdoor dining table. In the distance is a second and distinct outdoor dining room, complete with roofed, wood-burning pizza oven.

DRESSING UP GARDEN STRUCTURES TRANSFORMS THEM FROM MERELY FUNCTIONAL
ITEMS TO ONES THAT ARE FULL OF MEANING.

structures

Arbors, gazebos, and decks made of distressed or weather-worn wood add layers of history to the garden. The line and form of a structure can echo the home's roofline, thus extending architecture into the garden. Plants themselves can be used decoratively; vines grow lushly in our moist, mild climate, climbing quickly to spangle arbors, gates, or fences. You can add humor or color by topping posts and beams with pots, fanciful caps, or birdhouses. Heat up a shady terrace by paving with bright Moroccan tiles, or emphasize a Northwest sense of place by using naturally graying shingles on a fence or retaining wall.

Create personal sanctuaries within your garden, filling them with cherished objects that stir memories of favorite travels or of loved ones. Nooks in a wall, shadow boxes mounted on a fence, or sheltered corners of the garden can be used as small shrines to display such collections.

The mistiness of a seaside summer morning is captured in this Whidbey Island garden. The picket fence is painted the blazing blue of sea and sky at mid-day, and a wicker bench is topped with a metal arbor with swirls of leaves and branches too delicate to stop the eye or block the view.

right A mosaic snake slithers more than 20 feet through artist Claire Dohna's garden on Vashon Island, providing a pebbled pathway for passage through raised planting beds. The blues and greens of the diamond back rattler accent the blue of the sky and the chartreuse shades of garden foliage. below When faced with a bare shingled wall in this garden, artist Sue Skelly wove branches of Western red cedar into tapering curves attached to copper tubing. The frond-shaped trellises now serve as art and plant support at once.
{CORCORAN GARDEN, BAINBRIDGE ISLAND}

right A gate is made into an imposing architectural feature when flanked by pillars topped with highly glazed burgundy pots, each holding a single spreading hosta. The drama is in the strong and simple shapes of pillar, pot, and plant, and in the fact that the matching hostas are elevated to eye-level.

esources

growing fields

THE NORTHWEST'S GROWING FIELDS ARE FABULOUS PLACES TO GATHER IDEAS FOR YOUR OWN GARDEN DESIGNS.

Seeing field-grown "crops" of ornamental trees, shrubs, herbs, and perennials—many in display gardens—can help you learn about new varieties (imagine 400 cultivars of your favorite plant in one place), assess the color or form of flowers in bloom, or get an idea of a mature tree's appearance. Best of all, you'll meet inspiring experts who want to share their horticultural knowledge.

Some of these destinations regularly welcome tourists; others require a bit more planning. Always phone ahead to confirm your visit. And bring a camera and notepad—you'll want to record everything!

british columbia

BLUESTEM ORNAMENTAL GRASSES
1949 Fife Road, Christina Lake, B.C. V0H 1E3
(250) 447-6363 Call for appointment

Located in B.C.'s southern interior, Bluestem specializes in more than 50 ornamental grasses. Owner Jim Brockmeyer's display garden illustrates the mature size and flowering habit of grasses, paired with many companion plants.

PHOENIX PERENNIALS NURSERY
3380 No. 6 Road, Richmond, B.C. V6V 1P3
(604) 270-4133 Seasonal hours
www.phoenixperennials.com

Garden designer Clare Philips started Phoenix Perennials to grow unusual perennials for her clients. Now she maintains nearly 700 species of hardy perennials, along with four stunning display areas: yellow and white borders, which mingle together; a peach-mauve-purple border with its plum-colored ribbon of flowers; and a multihued shade bed.

oregon

ADELMAN PEONY GARDENS
5690 Brooklake Road NE, Salem, OR 97305
(503) 393-6185 Call for hours
www.peonyparadise.com

With nearly 30,000 individual plants in their Willamette Valley growing fields, Jim and Carol Adelman are indeed passionate about peonies. In addition to 200-plus varieties, they offer "intersectionals"—crosses between tree and herbaceous peonies. Special events are featured during the May and June bloom season.

FERGUSON'S FRAGRANT NURSERY
21763 French Prairie Road NE, St. Paul, OR 97137
(503) 633-4585 Open daily
www.fragrantnursery.com

This full-service nursery has glorious display gardens that feature a wide array of growing conditions. Ferguson's grows and sells fragrant plants including heliotrope, lavender, lilac, roses, viburnum, and more.

HEIRLOOM ROSES
24062 NE Riverside Drive, St. Paul, OR 97137
(503) 538-1576 Open daily
www.heirloomroses.com

A visit to Heirloom Roses' three display gardens is especially intoxicating from May to August, when more than 1,500 varieties of new and antique roses are blooming. Own-root and fragrant roses are featured, as are design ideas for English and cottage-style gardening.

SCHREINER'S IRIS GARDENS
3625 Quinaby Road NE, Salem, OR 97303
(503) 393-3232 or (800) 525-2367 Call for hours
www.schreinersgardens.com

In May and early June, hundreds of acres of irises bloom at Schreiner's, from the deepest black to pure white, fire red to azure blue, glowing copper to velvety purple.

SWAN ISLAND DAHLIAS
995 NW 22nd Avenue, Canby, OR 97013
(503) 266-7711 or (800) 410-6540 Call for hours
www.dahlias.com

Swan Island has come a long way from its roadside dahlia stand outside Portland to being the largest grower in the United States. Forty acres of fields are on display here from early August through the first frost.

If you swoon every time a whiff of lavender catches your nose, a visit to a lavender farm will help you learn more about these fragrant plants. {PURPLE HAZE LAVENDER FARM, 180 Bell Bottom Road, Sequim, WA 98382, (888) 852-6560. www.purplehazelavender.com}

washington

A & D NURSERY
6808 180th SE, Snohomish, WA 98296
(360) 668-9690 Call for hours
www.adpeonies.com

More than 1,000 favorite and hard-to-find varieties of peonies, daylilies, and hostas grow in this country garden. There's an inspiring selection of herbaceous and tree peonies, best seen in May and June. The nursery features one of the region's only official daylily displays for the American Hemerocallis Society, best seen in July. And the Hosta Walk is in a lush woodland setting.

AITKEN'S SALMON CREEK GARDEN
608 NW 119th Street, Vancouver, WA 98685
(360) 573-4472 Call for hours
www.flowerfantasy.net

Self-guided tours are offered from early April until July through more than 4 acres of dwarf, intermediate, standard, and tall bearded irises; Japanese irises; and species irises. Fields are organized by type and planted alphabetically; ask to see Aitken's own introductions.

B & D LILIES/SNOW CREEK DAYLILY GARDENS
284566 Hwy. 101 South, Port Townsend, WA 98368
(360) 765-4342 or 765-4341 Call for hours
www.bdlilies.com

Known for its enormous selection of all types of lilies, B & D's working farm and display gardens are open for self-guided tours mid-June to mid-August. Daylilies peak in mid-July, and the Oriental lilies peak by mid-August.

CEDARBROOK HERB FARM
1345 South Sequim Avenue, Sequim, WA 98382
(360) 683-7733 Open daily
www.cedarbrookherbfarm.com

Started in 1967 in the sunny Sequim-Dungeness Valley, this is Washington's oldest herb farm. Of Cedarbrook's 12 acres, 2 are open for year-round visits. During July and August you'll appreciate the region's ideal conditions for lavender cultivation. Petals Garden Café is on the premises for the hungry garden tourist.

COUNTRY GARDENS
36735 SE David Powell Road, Fall City, WA 98024
(425) 222-5616 Call for hours
www.nwlink.com/~dafox/

This small business propagates more than 200 hydrangea species and cultivars. Most hail from Europe, along with a few South American selections. July and August are the best months to view the shrubs in bloom.

PELINDABA LAVENDER
33 Hawthorne Lane, Friday Harbor, WA 98250
(360) 378-4248 Call for hours
www.pelindaba.com

View 20 varieties of lavender growing in the display gardens, including 2 acres of growing crops. On many weekends, you can take a guided tour of the gardens and production facility to see how Pelindaba produces essential oils for its 45 culinary, body, and bath products.

ROOZENGAARDE
15867 Beaver Marsh Road, Mt. Vernon, WA 98273
(800) 732-3266 Call for hours
www.tulips.com

The Roozen family business of tulips, daffodils, and irises covers Skagit Valley with more than 1,200 acres of field blooms and 8 acres of greenhouses—an expansive full-color production. Visit March through May to see mass plantings of favorite and unusual tulips, daffodils, and other bulbs.

SUNDQUIST NURSERY
3809 NE Sawdust Hill Road, Poulsbo, WA 98370
(360) 779-6343 Call for hours

Nils and Kristen Sundquist operate a wholesale ornamental grass nursery on 3 acres in Poulsbo. On Open Garden days, you can tour the display gardens planted around their 1928 farmhouse, enjoying the ornamental grass border ringed in Eatonville stone and the inspiring plant pairings.

hospitality

Many of the Northwest's finest inns and wineries have created lush gardens that entice visitors and enhance their experience. Restaurants with enough room may grow their own herbs and vegetables to ensure freshness and quality.

This is just a small sampling of the many wonderful gardens created by innkeepers, winemakers, and restaurateurs. Some places offer garden tours for guests who are not staying or dining on the premises; others have no set guidelines. But if you have the time, why not stay a while?

The garden beds at Sooke Harbour House are filled with an enticing mix of edible and ornamental plants. The restaurant serves only food that can be garden-grown or locally obtained, and features many dishes inspired by First Nations cuisine. This hillside garden slopes down to the ocean and is planted with a mix of daylilies, Calendula officinalis, Malva moschata, daylilies, and Monarda didyma—all of which find their way onto the restaurant menu. {SOOKE HARBOUR HOUSE, 1528 Whiffen Spit Road, Sooke, B.C. V0S 1N0, (250) 642-3421. www.sookeharbourhouse.com}

british columbia

GUISACHAN HOUSE RESTAURANT
1060 Cameron Avenue, Kelowna, B.C. V1W 4M3
(250) 862-9368 Open daily
www.worldclasscatering.com

This home (the name means "blaze of fir" in Gaelic) was once a summer residence for the Earl and Countess of Aberdeen. Today, there is an award-winning restaurant as well as a 2½-acre Victorian garden with a cedar allée, cobblestone walkways, two gazebos, a rose arbor, and butterfly gardens.

SUMMERHILL PYRAMID WINERY
4870 Chute Lake Road, Kelowna, B.C. V1W 4M3
(250) 764-8000 or (800) 667-3538 Call for hours
www.summerhill.bc.ca

A 65-acre certified organic vineyard, Summerhill Pyramid Winery overlooks the Okanagan Valley. Founder Stephen Cipes designed Summerhill's World Peace Park, which features a waterfall, a koi pond, and flower-filled gardens.

TUSCAN FARM GARDENS
24453 60th Avenue, Langley, B.C. V2Z 2G5
(604) 530-1997 Call for hours
www.tuscanfarmgardens.com

This 80-acre family estate and B&B is located in the heart of the Fraser Valley. Lavender and echinacea are celebrated in seasonal festivals and featured in Tuscan Farm skin products. There are secret gardens; rose arbors; and medicinal, moon, and tea gardens. Afternoon tea is served in the Bistro.

oregon

BETHEL HEIGHTS FARM BED & BREAKFAST
6055 Bethel Heights Road NW, Salem, OR 97304
(503) 364-7688 Call for hours
www.oregon-b-and-b.com

Leo and Ervina Anderson run a two-suite B&B in the heart of their family winery, Stand Sure Vineyard. They have an Oriental garden, a St. Francis garden, and a small fruit orchard to supply the gourmet kitchen. Across the road is the Bethel Heights Vineyard, whose gardens blend into the vineyard allée (6060 Bethel Heights Road NW; (503) 581-2262; www.bethelheights.com).

COLUMBIA GORGE HOTEL
4000 Westcliff Drive, Hood River, OR 97031
(541) 386-5566 or (800) 345-1921 Open daily
www.columbiagorgehotel.com

Built in 1921 in 18th-century style, this historic hotel and its grounds are situated above a rushing waterfall. It has 11 acres of beautifully landscaped gardens, which are undergoing renovation to complement the inn's architecture.

KING ESTATE WINERY
80854 Territorial Road, Eugene, OR 97405
(541) 942-9874 or (800) 884-4441
Open daily, Memorial Day to October (or by appointment)
www.kingestate.com

Lavender fields welcome you to King Estate, where you can tour expansive culinary gardens with herbs, greens, and vegetables used for events and tastings. The gardens also feature several types of cane berries and more than 100 fruit trees.

McMENAMINS EDGEFIELD
2126 SW Halsey Street, Troutdale, OR 97060
(503) 669-8610 or (800) 669-8610 Open daily
www.mcmenamins.com

Built in 1911 as the Multnomah County Poor Farm, Edgefield is now on the National Register of Historic Places. Thirty-eight landscaped acres of trees, shrubs, perennials, and herbs surround the 114-room inn and the Black Rabbit Restaurant. The grounds also feature a 3½-acre Pinot Gris vineyard and a greenhouse.

REX HILL VINEYARDS AND WINERY
30835 North Highway 99 West, Newberg, OR 97132
(503) 538-0666 or (800) 739-4455 Call for hours
www.rexhill.com

Rex Hill is a former fruit farm whose original brick nut-drying plant has been rebuilt into a tasting room that houses owners Paul Hart and Jan Jacobsen's extensive Northwest art collection. The grounds are elegantly landscaped with a profusion of perennials and seasonal annuals, terraced into an outdoor amphitheater for picnicking guests.

SPRINGBROOK HAZELNUT FARM
30295 North Highway 99 West, Newberg, OR 97132
(503) 538-4606 or (800) 793-8528 Call for hours
www.nutfarm.com

This peaceful Yamhill County estate encompasses four Craftsman-style buildings nestled among 10 acres of gardens, complete with huge old trees and a 1-acre pond edged with yellow irises. Sixty acres of hazelnut orchards surround the gardens, and each spring more than 15,000 daffodils bloom in the adjacent meadow.

washington

COUNTRY COTTAGE OF LANGLEY
215 Sixth Street, Langley, WA 98260
(360) 221-8709 or (800) 713-3860 Call for hours
www.acountrycottage.com

Located in the heart of the Whidbey Island village of Langley is this charming cluster of six private cottages, each with a different theme. The cottages face a central gazebo garden overlooking Puget Sound. Orchard trees, raised English garden beds planted with bulbs and perennials, and a vibrant goldenchain tree enhance the setting.

Several specialty gardens have been planted by local Master Gardeners.

FRENCH ROAD FARM COTTAGE AND HOME BY THE SEA
2388 East Sunlight Beach Road, Clinton, WA 98236
(360) 321-2964 Call for hours
www.homebytheseacottages.com

Linda Walsh has designed French Road Farm Cottage for year-round color and fragrance, with a perennial border that begins with silvery whites at one end, moves through vivid oranges and deep purples at the center, and finishes with pink, white, and gray. Home by the Sea's windswept landscape incorporates natives and plants that provide habitat for coastal wildlife.

GASLIGHT INN
1727 15th Avenue, Seattle, WA 98122
(206) 325-3654 Call for hours.
www.gaslight-inn.com

A pair of side-by-side Four Square homes built in the early 1900s, Gaslight Inn is an urban getaway on Seattle's Capitol Hill. The courtyard garden features a koi pond designed with basalt columns and unusual perennials. The secluded swimming pool and terrace are planted with giant palms, banana trees, and hardy vines.

SERAFINA RESTAURANT
2043 Eastlake Avenue East, Seattle, WA 98102
(206) 323-0807 Open daily
www.serafinaseattle.com

Susan Kaufman's country Italian restaurant and bar has served a loyal following in Seattle's Eastlake neighborhood for more than a decade. The Serafina Kitchen Garden (at 2015 Franklin Avenue East) is where chef John Neumark harvests organic herbs and heirloom vegetables.

THORNEWOOD CASTLE INN AND GARDENS
8601 North Thorne Lane SW, Lakewood, WA 98498
(253) 584-4393 Open by appointment
www.thornewoodcastle.com

Built in 1908 by Tacoma financier Chester A. Thorne, Thornewood Castle is now the private residence of Wayne and Deanna Robinson, who are restoring the Gothic Tudor mansion and Olmsted-designed landscape. The sunken English garden, fern garden with statuary, and grand European fountain are special features.

WILLOW BROOK FARM COTTAGE
12600 Miller Road NE, Bainbridge Island, WA 98110
(206) 842-8034 Call for hours
www.willowbrookfarm.com

Willow Brook Farm Cottage offers sweeping views of green pastures and 25 acres of certified organic farmland. All food served at the cottage comes from the farm, which grows many crops, from berries to apples, vegetables, and herbs. Enjoy the annual and perennial cutting beds.

Four Portland women had tremendous influence on 20th-century Northwest horticulture.

portland gardeners

Lady Anne McDonald and Jane Platt (née the Kerr sisters), Lilla Leach, and Rae Selling Berry may have had different interests, but they had one important thing in common: Each of the gardens they left behind has excellent winter-flowering shrubs. The wise will take note.

the kerr sisters

Born not long after their father started to develop his Portland estate at Elk Rock, Anne and Jane Kerr (later Lady Anne McDonald and Jane Platt) were surrounded by great gardening minds: their horticulturally minded father, Peter Kerr, who brought back plants from his frequent international travels; John Charles Olmsted, who spent 10 years establishing the layout of the estate's gardens; and John Misch, the family's resident gardener. By the time the sisters married and established their own landscapes, each had Northwest garden style in her bones. Both were long-standing members of the Portland Garden Club, both developed outstanding private gardens, and both were actively involved with the garden at Elk Rock for life.

Among them, the three gardens—Elk Rock, McDonald's, and Platt's—contained a fantastic array of plants from all categories. Many were quite rare, but the visitors who saw them created the demand that motivated the nursery industry to make them available.

Lady McDonald had broad garden tastes. Like her father, she gardened for most of her 95 years. She was particularly fond of winter-flowering shrubs.

Jane Platt progressed through horticultural phases. At one time or another she focused on everything from alliums and species rhododendrons to stewartias, magnolias, and a range of winter-flowering shrubs. During the last decade of her life, she developed a rock garden that many considered the crown jewel of her private landscape.

The Garden at Elk Rock was renamed Elk Rock Gardens of the Bishop's Close when it was given to the Episcopal Diocese of Oregon in 1959.

ELK ROCK GARDENS OF THE BISHOP'S CLOSE
11800 SW Military Lane
Portland, OR 97219
(503) 636-5613 or (800) 452-2562
Open daily 8 A.M. to 5 P.M.; closed some holidays
www.diocese-oregon.org/index.htm

lilla leach

It was a marriage made in heaven: She was a plant-collecting botanist, he (a pharmacist) was a pretty fair mule skinner. Together, Lilla and John Leach led pack mules over the Oregon landscape and collected native plants in the early part of the last century.

Browse through any good Northwest flora and you'll see a couple of marks of their success: the lovely evergreen *Iris innominata;* and a small, heathlike shrub with purple-tinged rose-colored flowers called *Kalmiopsis leachiana.* The *Kalmiopsis,* which the Leaches found in a remote part of southwest Oregon's Siskiyou Mountains in 1930, is one of just two members of its genus.

During the 1930s, the Leaches started work on their personal garden, Sleepy Hollow. Arranged by habitat, it lies naturally over creek and slope, ridge and dell. Lilla Leach included plenty of exotics in her garden as well as natives. Look for numerous collections here: irises, ferns, rock plants, winter bloomers, grasses, cactus, succulents, and wildflowers.

LEACH BOTANICAL GARDEN
6704 SE 122nd Avenue, Portland, OR 97236
(503) 823-9503 Call for hours
www.parks.ci.portland.or.us/Parks/LeachBotanicalGar.htm

rae selling berry

had a passion for plants— particularly ones that few people had ever seen. She helped fund the expeditions of legendary explorers like Joseph Rock and Frank Kingdon-Ward, and received seeds from them in exchange. Consequently, she was able to grow species of rhododendrons and primulas that had never flowered under Northwestern light, and she developed plant collections that others could only dream about.

Berry herself went on expeditions in search of alpine plants, expanding her remarkable rock garden in the process. She loved challenges: Propagation of Oregon's difficult native primrose, *Primula cusickiana,* was her pet project.

The microhabitats in what is now Berry Botanic Garden include springs and creeks, a ravine, a meadow, a spectacular (in spring) rock garden, a cattail marsh, and a bog garden complete with native carnivorous plants; pay special attention to woodland ground covers here.

BERRY BOTANIC GARDEN
11505 SW Summerville Avenue
Portland, OR 97219
(503) 636-4112 Call for appointment
www.berrybot.org

THE DISCOVERY OF A NEW NURSERY IS ONE OF THE GARDENER'S GREATEST PLEASURES.

specialty nurseries

Often tucked at the end of a country lane or known only to locals, small specialty nurseries can contain a surprising number of unusual or rare plants. And although we may tell ourselves that we're "just looking," it's hard to go home empty-handed.

The Northwest is dotted with such out-of-the-way gems, selling everything from roses to herbs, grasses to alpines. A small nursery might not have an extensive Web site or full-color catalogue, but there is something it is likely to have: passionate plant lovers dedicated to growing the best plants they can. And although they may be busy potting up seedlings, labeling plants, or keeping the stock watered when you visit, chances are they'll find the time to stop and talk plants with you.

alaska

ED'S EDIBLE LANDSCAPING
17300 Andreanoff Drive, Juneau, AK 99801
(907) 789-2299 Call for hours

Ed Buyarski is a landscaper, a primrose grower, and the current president of the American Primrose Society. In his small nursery, Buyarski grows and sells more than 50 species of primulas; his nursery and display gardens offer an education about the varieties of *Primula*, peonies, Japanese maples, and fruit that can be grown in southeast Alaska's wet, four-season climate.

IN THE GARDEN
3021 De Armoun Road, Anchorage, AK 99516
(907) 345-9168 or (907) 346-4246 Call for hours

Co-owners Sally Arant, a landscape architect and garden designer, and plantswoman Lorri Abel started In the Garden because they couldn't find the unique plants they wanted elsewhere. The demonstration garden features a wide selection of grasses, shade plants, and unusual foliage plants; take note of Arant's great companion plant pairings in the border.

TRYCK NURSERY
3625 Rabbit Creek Road, Anchorage, AK 99516
(907) 345-2507 Call for hours

In his seasonal nursery, Doug Tryck sells unusual trees, shrubs, vines, and perennials. His display gardens are located on 2½ south-facing acres. See a number of planting demonstrations in natural settings, including a herbaceous border, a Japanese garden, and an espalier "living fence." Take note of the rock, bog, and water gardens ideas, too.

british columbia

ABKHAZI GARDEN
1964 Fairfield Road, Victoria, B.C. V9E 2H2
(250) 479-8053 or (250) 598-8096 Call for hours
www.conservancy.bc.ca

The Abkhazi Garden is a heritage property created in the late 1940s by Russian Prince and Princess Abkhazi. The garden contrasts nature's glacial and woodland elements, and features native Garry oaks, ornamental evergreens, mature rhododendrons, rock and alpine plants, naturalized bulbs, Japanese maples, and weeping conifers.

FREE SPIRIT NURSERY
20405 32nd Avenue, Langley, B.C. V2Z 2C7
(604) 533-7373 Call for hours
www.plantlovers.com

Lambert and Marjanne Vrijmoed arrived in the Fraser Valley from Holland in the early 1990s to practice landscape design. Today, their award-winning venture includes grasses, epimediums, digitalis, woodland plants, shrubs, vines, and "new wave" perennials inspired by Lambert's mentor Piet Oudolf.

PACIFIC RIM NATIVE PLANT NURSERY
44305 Old Orchard Road, Chilliwack, B.C. V2R 1A9
(604) 792-9279 Call for hours
www.hillkeep.ca

Patricia and Paige Woodward are a mother-and-daughter team whose home and nursery are situated on a small cultivated patch inside the 80-acre Hillkeep Nature Reserve at the top of Chilliwack Mountain. Their specialties include an extraordinary list of bulbs, vines, alpine plants, grasses, ferns, trees, and shrubs.

Run by the Savin family on Salt Spring Island, The Plant Farm has 4 acres of display gardens showcasing many of the varied plants grown and sold at the nursery. Here, a variegated box-wood hedge curves past a bed of assorted euphorbias and the bamboo Borinda angustissima, and into a clearing ringed with conifers. On the other side of the path, a spinning gum (Eucalyptus perriniana) rises out of a bed of assorted peonies. {THE PLANT FARM, 177 Vesuvius Bay Road, Salt Spring Island, B.C. V8K 1K3, (250) 537-5995. www.theplantfarm.ca}

SELECT ROSES
22771 38th Avenue, Langley, B.C. V2Z 2G9
(604) 530-5786 Call for hours

Brad Jalbert grows and hybridizes a huge selection of full-size and miniature roses at the family cottage nursery, including 30 of his own introduction. The magnificent display gardens have more than 700 mature roses. This is an official demonstration garden for the Canadian Rose Society.

oregon

CISTUS DESIGN NURSERY/HOGAN & SANDERSON
22711 NW Gillihan Road, Sauvie Island, OR 97231
(503) 621-2233 or (503) 282-7706 Call for hours
www.cistus.com

Located on Portland's Sauvie Island, Cistus specializes in plants that thrive in the maritime Northwest but hail from Southern Hemisphere, Asian, and Mediterranean climates. Sean Hogan and Parker Sanderson are plant aficionados who display their passion in several intoxicating borders.

JOY CREEK NURSERY
20300 NW Watson Road, Scappoose, OR 97056
(503) 543-7474 Open daily March through October
www.joycreek.com

Mike Smith and Maurice Horn operate their dream nursery offering more than 2,000 perennials and glorious display gardens that encompass 4 acres. If you are looking for drought-tolerant plants, check out the dry border garden for ideas. And if clematis is your weakness, be prepared for a special treat.

NORTHWEST GARDEN NURSERY
86813 Central Road, Eugene, OR 97402
(541) 935-3915 Call for hours

Ernie and Marietta O'Byrne specialize in rock garden plants and out-of-the-ordinary herbaceous perennials for sun and shade. Visitors are drawn to their extensive collector's garden, an acre-plus of luxurious perennial borders in sun and semishade; woodlands underplanted with a tapestry of ground covers, hellebores, ferns, primulas, and meconopsis; a rock garden with rare alpines; and an ornamental grass garden mixed with hot-colored plants.

washington

BAMBOO GARDENS OF WASHINGTON
196th Avenue NE and Highway 202 East
  (Redmond-Fall City Road), Redmond, WA 98074
(425) 868-5166 Open daily
www.BambooGardensWA.com

This specialty nursery is the place to learn about bamboo, as it features more than 45 varieties of ornamental and timber bamboo. Wander through the rustling groves that illustrate mature bamboo habits. View several displays of bamboo paired with great companion plants.

CULTUS BAY NURSERY
7568 Cultus Bay Road, Clinton, WA 98236
(360) 579-2329 Call for hours

Mary and Tom Fisher live in a lovely Victorian-style farmhouse on Whidbey Island, surrounded by English cottage gardens and their specialty nursery. The inviting display beds include a herbaceous border of trees, shrubs, grasses, and perennials. A hellebore growing bed stocks the nursery. Enjoy touring the grounds and small pond, and look for ornamental art and garden accessories by local craftspeople.

DIG NURSERY
19028 Vashon Highway SW, Vashon Island, WA
(206) 463-5096 Open daily

Artist and plantswoman Sylvia Matlock has blended her two passions at DIG. The entry drive is decked out with an attention-grabbing display bed filled with a dazzling selection of annuals, specialty perennials, and shrubs. You'll also find garden art from an astonishing variety of artisans and a big commitment to container gardening, with great pots and Sylvia's glorious plant combinations.

EMERY'S GARDEN
2829 164th Street SW, Lynnwood, WA 98037
(425) 743-4555 Open daily
www.emerysgarden.com

Emery's has one of the largest and most diverse tree and shrub offerings in the region, with a special emphasis on Japanese maples and conifers. The nursery has restored the property's peaceful and secluded Japanese meditation garden and ponds. An aviary with exotic fowl will delight youngsters, and the perennial and grass borders will wow their parents. Other displays illustrate plant combinations, water features, specimen trees, and garden artwork.

FAIRIE PERENNIAL AND HERB GARDENS NURSERY
6236 Elm Street SE, Tumwater, WA 98501
(360) 754-9249 Open daily February through October
www.fairiegardens.net

You might visit to purchase plants, but you'll stay to tour the fantastical gardens that fill this ½-acre site. Continuous paths lead you on a horticultural adventure through several theme gardens, including those planted with culinary interest, water features, fragrant plants, and medieval imagery.

HERONSWOOD NURSERY
7530 NE 288th Street, Kingston, WA 98346
(360) 297-4172 Call for hours
www.heronswood.com

A plant collector's Mecca, Heronswood Nursery is the creation of Daniel Hinkley and Robert Jones, who have spent a dozen years creating a nursery of uncommon plants and extensive gardens. The landscape is planted with rare trees, shrubs, perennials, and vines, thriving beneath the evergreen under story. A bog garden, complete with Little & Lewis sculptures and columns, transports you to another time. Visit during special "Garden Open" dates or arrange a personally guided tour for a fee.

NAYLOR CREEK NURSERY
2610 West Valley Road, Chimacum, WA 98325
(360) 732-4983 Call for hours
www.naylorcreek.com

Jack Hirsch and Gary Lindheimer specialize in more than 800 hosta varieties and many other shade-tolerant perennials, grown in their small nursery on the Olympic Peninsula. Their plants are shown in raised beds and containers, which offer you a great way to see the nuances and patterning of these lush, leafy plants.

PIRIFORMIS
1051 North 35th Street, Seattle, WA 98103
(206) 632-1760 Open daily
www.piriformis.com

The displays frequently change at Tory Galloway's postage stamp-size nursery in Seattle's Fremont neighborhood, but you'll always find inspiration there. Her creative combinations and whimsical artifacts prove that drought tolerant does not have to be dull.

STEAMBOAT ISLAND NURSERY
8424 Steamboat Island Road, Olympia, WA 98502
(360) 866-2516 Call for hours
www.olywa.net/steamboat

Laine McLaughlin is an environmentalist and horticulturist who tries to propagate every plant that catches her fancy. The result is an uncommon selection of trees, shrubs, grasses, perennials, and annuals. Steamboat Island's display gardens are continually evolving, featuring some deer-resistant and drought tolerant plants (for shade and sun), a winter garden, and container planting ideas.

TOWER PERENNIAL GARDENS
4010 East Jamieson Road, Spokane, WA 99223
(509) 448-6778 Call for hours

In Spokane, Alan and Susan Tower grow and sell perennials, dwarf conifers, shrubs, rock garden and alpine plants, bonsai, roses, and aquatic plants. They have developed extensive display gardens on 8 pastoral acres, surrounding a century-old rustic barn and farmhouse. Alan is actively involved in the American Hosta Society, so you'll want to explore the 500-plus hosta varieties on display.

surprising settings

Sometimes great gardens pop up in unexpected places. After you've exhausted the Northwest's nurseries, arboretums, and botanical gardens, journey a bit farther down the road to these offbeat locations.

In southeast Alaska's Mendenhall Valley, you'll discover an otherworldly landscape at Glacier Gardens Rainforest Adventure {7600 Glacier Highway, Juneau, AK 99801, (907) 790-3377. www.glaciergardens.com}. This 50-acre site is in a temperate rain forest on the side of Thunder Mountain. The display gardens are planted with Japanese maples, dogwoods, rhododendrons, azaleas, ferns, and mosses. Glacier Gardens' entrance is embellished with 30 fantastical trees—felled Sitka spruces and Western hemlocks that have been buried into the ground; the roots form planted "bowls" filled with seasonal floral and ivy displays.

alaska

MANN LEISER GREENHOUSE AT RUSSIAN JACK SPRINGS PARK
5200 DeBarr Road, Anchorage, AK 99508
(907) 343-4717 Call for hours

At this municipal greenhouse, Anchorage Parks & Recreation horticulturists grow the many bedding plants that beautify city streets. The tropical house and solarium offer a warm green refuge when nothing else is growing; the display is especially dazzling during the winter holidays. In the summer, be sure to visit the All-American Selection trial bed outside the greenhouse to see new varieties of vegetables and annuals.

british columbia

PARK & TILFORD GARDENS
440-333 Brooksbank Avenue, North Vancouver, B.C. V7J 3S8
(604) 984-8200 Open daily

This surprising 2½-acre treasure, located adjacent to a shopping mall in North Vancouver, is well worth the visit. Nine theme gardens are integrated into this landscape. Displays of roses, natives, Oriental plants, white flowers, yellow flowers, herbs, annuals, townhouse, and magnolia/rhododendron are especially inspiring for those who garden in smaller settings.

oregon

DARLINGTONIA BOTANICAL WAYSIDE
84505 U.S. Highway 101 South, Florence, OR 97439
Open daily
www.ohwy.com/or/o/orparks.htm

The Darlingtonia Wayside is located north of the oceanside town of Florence, accessible via a boardwalk that leads out to a marshy bog. This is the natural habitat of our native carnivorous plants *Darlingtonia californica* (cobra lily or pitcher plant) and *Drosera rotundifolia*. From spring to early fall, you can watch the plants eat insects that fall into them.

washington

ROSEBAR METAL GARDEN ART
20640 Skagit City Road, Mount Vernon, WA 98273
(360) 445-2294 Call for hours
www.rosebar.net

Artist and welder Mary Taylor is known for her ornamental metal trellises, arbors, finials, and obelisks. Her studio and welding shop are housed in a rustic old barn; outside, you'll find a series of highly textured gardens filled with perennials, woody plants, and, of course, flowering vines that she encourages to climb on her embellished garden structures.

SOUTH SEATTLE COMMUNITY COLLEGE ARBORETUM
6000 16th Avenue SW, Seattle, WA 98106
(206) 764-5396 Open daily

Within this 6-acre teaching arboretum is a fabulous dwarf conifer display that demonstrates more than 100 cultivars suitable for smaller landscapes. The collection has been established with the help of conifer experts Robert and Dianne Fincham, owners of Coenosium Gardens, a mail-order nursery in Eatonville, Washington. Take note of the wide variety of conifer colors, forms, and textures in this unusual collection.

index

Boldface numbers refer to photos and captions.

photography credits

Wayne Aldridge: 3 bottom right, 44 left, 178 top, 179 bottom middle
Scott Atkinson: 52 right
Janice Dodd/Berry Botanical Garden: 185 bottom
Rob Cardillo: 58 top left
Philip Clayton-Thompson: 67 bottom, 78 top, 144 bottom, 163 top right, 171 bottom left
Patrick Johns/Corbis: 113 bottom left
Robin B. Cushman: 37 bottom, 66, 67 top left, top right; 118 top right, 120, 123 bottom left, top right; 132 left, 133 top left, right; 137 top right, 143, 150 top left, 152 right, 162 bottom, 166, 169 middle left
Andrew Drake: 27 bottom left, 28, 64 top, 78 bottom, 79 right, 98 bottom, 111 bottom left, 115 left, 127 top left, 147 bottom right, 150 top right, bottom right; 154 top, 158 top left, bottom left; 164 top left, top right, bottom right; 165, 177 top right
judywhite/GardenPhotos.com: 150 bottom left, 157 top left, 163 bottom left
Larry Geddis: 23 top, 102 bottom middle, 110 top
Adam Gibbs: 51 top, 52 left, 68, 102 bottom left, bottom right, 106 bottom right, 134 top left, 146 bottom left, 167 bottom left
Fiona Gilsenan: 25 top, 49 bottom right, 74, 99 bottom right, 113 top left, 117 left, 121 bottom, 125 bottom left, top left, bottom right; 128, 164 middle, 173 right
Harold Greer/Greer Gardens: 115 right
Jerry Harpur: 167 bottom right, 173 bottom left
Lynne Harrison: 19, 31 bottom, 38, 39, 103 bottom left, 131 bottom, 134 bottom left, 135 top, 145 bottom, 146 bottom middle left, 147 bottom left, 161 bottom, 168
Richard Hartlage: 23 bottom, 26 bottom left, bottom right; 49 bottom left, 80 bottom, 86 right, 90 bottom, 96, 103 bottom right, 119 top left, bottom; 126, 137 top left, 160 bottom left
Fred Hirschmann: 2 bottom left, 4, 20, 57 top left, 58 bottom, 127 bottom left, 179 bottom right, 188
Randi Hirschmann: 169 bottom left
Saxon Holt: 114 right
Michael Jensen: 92, 93 bottom left, top right, bottom right; 172, 175
Jacqueline Koch: 107, 112 bottom, 122, 155 right, 176
Debby Van Meter/Leach Botanical Garden: 184, 185 top
Janet Loughrey: 2 bottom middle, 22, 26 top, 27 bottom middle, 29 bottom left, 45 bottom, 77 left, top right; 97 top left, 109 left, 115 bottom, 117 right, 118 bottom, 123 bottom right, 157 top right, 160 right, 163 top left, 170 left, 171 bottom right, 174 top right, bottom

Mary-Kate Mackey: 112 top
Allan Mandell: 2 top, 18, 27 bottom right, 40, 41, 42, 43 top, 61 top left, top right; 72, 73 bottom, 76 top, bottom; 77 middle right, 79 top, bottom; 82, 83, 97 top right, bottom; 100, 101, 111 bottom right, 116, 127 right, 138 right, 139 top, 140 right, 146 bottom right, 148,149, 156, 157 bottom right, 158 right, 159, 160 top left, 167 top right, 169 right, 170 right,173 top left, 174 top left
Charles Mann: 46, 47 top left, top right; 60, 62 top, 106 left
Jim McCausland: 9, 24, 121 top, 178 bottom left, 181
Sharron Milstein/Spindrift Photographics: 2 bottom right, 3 bottom left, 43 bottom, 48, 63 top left, top right; 65 bottom, 73 top, 94, 102 top, 103 bottom middle, 139 bottom, 144 top, 145 top, 146 top, 147 bottom middle, 171 top right
Terrence Moore: 26 bottom middle, 50, 153 top
Oregon State University Archives, Corvallis: 110 bottom
David McDonald/Photo Garden: 155 left, 167 top left
Norm Plate: 30, 32, 33, 47 bottom right, 51 bottom, 53, 56, 57 bottom left, right; 58 top right, 59, 65 top, 69, 75, 81, 84, 108 right, 109 right, 129 right, 135 bottom, 142 middle, 152 left, 153 middle, 154 bottom, 161 top, 162 top, 177 left, 178 bottom right, 179 bottom left, 182, 187
Sandra Lee Reha: 35 top left, 36, 95 top, 177 bottom right
Susan A. Roth: 34, 95 bottom,130, 178 bottom middle
France Ruffenach: 105 bottom
Jeff Shultz: 155 bottom
Siskiyou Rare Plant Nursery: 105 top
Peter Symcox: 21, 49 top, 90 top, 91 bottom, 141 middle, bottom
Martin Tessler: 35 bottom left, top right; 54, 55, 88, 89, 91 top, 108 left, 133 bottom left
Michael S. Thompson: 104, 114 left, 125 top left, 129 left, 142 top
Mark Turner: 1, 62 bottom, 70, 71, 111 top left, 118 top left, 119 top right, 124, 132 right, 134 right, 136, 151, 169 top left
Larry Ulrich: 6, 8, 11
Paddy Wales: 25 bottom, 29 top, bottom right; 31 top, 37 top right, 44 right, 45 top right, 61 bottom, 64 bottom, 85, 86 left, bottom; 98 top right, 99 top right, 131 top, 138 top left, bottom left, 140 top left, bottom left; 141 top, 157 bottom left, 163 bottom right
Lee Anne White: 169 top middle
Ben Woolsey: 113 bottom right

acknowledgments

The editors would like to thank the following for their contributions to *Gardening in the Northwest.*

Mark Albright—Department of Atmospheric Sciences, University of Washington, Seattle, WA
Doug Box—The Bamboo Farm, Salt Spring Island, B.C.
Bridget Biscotti Bradley
Scott Conner
Byron Cook and Sinclair Philips—Sooke Harbour House, Sooke, B.C.
Tina Dixon
Janice Dodd—Berry Botanic Garden, Portland, OR
Adrienne Edmonson—Vashon Allied Arts, Vashon Island, WA
Sue Eyre
Karen Fischer
Harold Greer—Greer Gardens, Eugene, OR
Claudia Groth—Whitney Farms, Independence, OR
Phyllis Gustafson
Ben Hammontree
Erica Harris—Clinton Bamboo, Seattle, WA
Junkoh Harui—Bainbridge Gardens, Bainbridge Island, WA
Dan Hinkley—Heronswood Nursery Ltd., Kingston, WA
Steve Hootman—Rhododendron Species Botanic Garden, Federal Way, WA
Robin Hopper and Judy Dyelle—Choisin Pottery, Metchosin, B.C.
Duane Kelly
Des Kennedy

Mareen and Art Kruckeberg
Rhoda Love
Jill and Peter MacDonald
Audrey Mak
Sylvia Matlock—Dig Nursery, Vashon Island, WA
Sara Mauritz—Friends of Elk Rock Gardens, Portland, OR
Jim McCann
Baldassare Mineo—Siskiyou Rare Plant Nursery, Medford, OR
Ciscoe Morris
Valerie Murray
Phoebe Noble
Brooke O'Brien
Joanie Parsons—Parsons Public Relations, Seattle, WA
Glen Patterson
David Platt
John and Jacki Ross
Jeff Savin—The Plant Farm, Salt Spring Island, B.C.
SoilSoup Compost Tea—Edmonds, WA
Peter Symcox
George Taylor—Oregon Climate Service, Oregon State University, Corvallis, OR
Cass Turnbull
Debby Van Meter—Leach Botanical Garden, Portland, OR
Glenn Withey and Charles Price